# EXECUTIVE INTELLIGENCE

# EXECUTIVE INTELLIGENCE

WHAT ALL GREAT LEADERS HAVE

## Justin Menkes

Collins

An Imprint of HarperCollinsPublishers

First Collins paperback edition published 2006

*Designed by Joel Avirom and Jason Snyder*

Library of Congress Cataloging-in-Publication Data has been applied for.

ISBN-10:  0-06-078188-2 (pbk.)
ISBN-13:  978-0-06-078188-0 (pbk.)

06 07 08 09 10 ❖/RRD  10 9 8 7 6 5 4 3 2 1

# FOR SUSAN

||||||||||||||||||

# Acknowledgments

Michael Mann: For his invaluable contributions to the writing of this book. Michael is a genius with words. I would not have wanted to do this project without him.

My colleagues at Spencer Stuart: It is an honor to work with such great people. Special thanks to Tom Neff, Jim Citrin, Dennis Carey, John Wood, and Joe Boccuzi for their gracious and very generous efforts on my behalf.

Bob Damon: For believing in me, and being such a true friend. I owe much of my career to the opportunities Bob made available to me.

Rafe Sagalyn: For his uncanny instincts, and incredible ability to make things happen. I couldn't ask for a better literary agent.

Marion Maneker: His terrific reputation within the publishing industry is well deserved. It was a pleasure to work with him.

# CONTENTS

# SECTION I:
# WHAT *IS* EXECUTIVE INTELLIGENCE—AN OVERVIEW

|||||||||||||||||||||

## CHAPTER 1

## CHAPTER 2

## CHAPTER 3

## CHAPTER 4

# SECTION IV:
# HOW DO YOU MEASURE EXECUTIVE INTELLIGENCE?

|||||||||||||||||||

## CHAPTER 15

## CHAPTER 16

## CHAPTER 17

# INTRODUCTION:
# The Unmistakable Signs of a Rising Star

Andrea Jung graduated from Princeton University in 1979 with a bachelor's degree in English literature, and took a job at Bloomingdale's, participating in its management-training program. After distinguishing herself at Bloomingdale's, she eventually took executive positions at I. Magnin and then Neiman Marcus. But in 1993, Avon "came calling," asking Jung to work as a marketing consultant. Within a year she was made head of Avon's product marketing division, with a primary mission—to help modernize the company.

Avon had been a successful, profitable company since it had been started in 1887, but by the early 1990s, the cosmetics company had badly slipped in the marketplace. Company research pointed to a persistent, potentially serious problem that had developed with the brand, which was viewed by many as a line of "cheap" cosmetics that only grandmothers wore.

This public perception and the company's lagging sales required that Avon make significant changes to improve its product lines and brand image. But one of the first, most crucial steps was to communicate this strategy to the local Avon sales representatives in order to help them understand and buy into the changes. Avon had been started as a company that helped women empower other women. It used a direct-sales approach that depended on local representatives who worked, often part-time, to sell the products to their friends and neighbors. Without the sales representatives' support, any change initiative that was passed down from corporate headquarters was doomed to failure.

Andrea Jung knew that this was where her mission had to begin. She had to help the Avon saleswomen understand and buy into the plan to upgrade the brand's positioning in the market. But this was no easy task. Although the company's market share was declining, many of the local saleswomen were still making decent money—money their families depended on.

One of the first major product changes to be instituted was the replacement of an older line of fragrance with a new, more expensive one. Andrea Jung explains further:

"When I first came into Avon, in a marketing role, the consumer research said that we were seen as being cheap. *Cheap* and *inexpensive* are different things. According to our research, this difference regarding our products had become blurred. So we needed to correct this image problem.

One of the first things we did was to introduce a new, higher-end fragrance line. The average Avon fragrance was selling for between $10 and $12, and our sales representatives were selling millions of units every year. And here we were coming to replace that with a new fragrance line that sold for $18.50.

There was tremendous negative resistance. All of our Avon Ladies worried that it was too expensive, and that they would lose all their Christmas money, because the old fragrance was something reliable that they were able to sell every year, particularly during the holidays. But we needed them to take this leap to modernize the company."

While market trends and research showed corporate management that they had a serious problem on their hands, Avon's front-line people found it hard to believe that the answer to the company's woes was to take away one of their most dependable selling items.

As a result, Jung was put in a difficult position. She knew that forcing the change through top-down edicts was likely to backfire, because she needed these Avon Ladies, "the faces of the company to its customers," to actually buy in, otherwise there was little hope that this strategy would be successfully executed in the field. This was particularly crucial, since the introduction of the new fragrance line was just the first in a planned series of similar product changes.

So Jung and her team personally met with groups of Avon Ladies and tried to explain the need to make these changes. Despite their rigorous presentation of market research data showing that the reps would make more money if they sold a more upscale product line, there was tremendous resistance. Many protested that the plan was a terrible idea and could not understand why management was trying to "upset the apple cart." As Jung recalls:

"I was looking around the room at all these frustrated faces and it suddenly dawned on me that these women were no different from our customers. After all, they were selling our products to their friends and family. So I asked them a simple question:

'How many of you really wear our fragrance? Forget about what you sell. Do you even use our products? Compared to the fragrance classics, do you keep coming back and using Avon?' The room was silent.

Once we explained our reasoning from a perspective that our representatives could understand, they realized what we were trying to do and why. They had to face up to the fact themselves that 'We're not even proud to wear the products we sell.' That was the key to getting them to see the need for our new strategy.

When we later heard that these same representatives had started saying to others around the company, 'I get what they [management] are trying to do'—that was the most important communication we could achieve. Because the spreading of support for this initiative had to come from them—only they could do it.

From there, a cascading understanding of the issue and the soundness of our solution began to flow through the company. That was a crucial turning point."

Jung's handling of this situation showed her to possess a particular, rather uncommon ability, and her talent was not lost on Avon's senior leadership. It was this type of highly skilled thinking that ultimately landed Jung in the top spot, becoming Avon's CEO after only six years at the company. Since Jung took charge in 1999, Avon's sales have jumped 45 percent, from $5.3 billion to nearly $8 billion; the company's stock has risen 164 percent, with five consecutive years of double-digit growth, including earnings growth of 25 percent between 2002 and 2005. Avon's turnaround is obvious and impressive.

Andrea Jung has become one of the most respected CEOs in the world, sitting on the board of directors for General Electric and the International Advisory Board for Salomon Smith Barney. The power of her clear thinking is readily apparent to anyone who meets her. Yet, she never went to business school nor had any traditional business training. So what is it about Andrea Jung and other exceptional executives that gives them such brilliant, instinctive business acumen? They obviously possess a rare kind of intelligence, one that is at the heart of star managerial performance. It is that intelligence that this book is all about.

# The Beginning

"*Everything he says makes sense—and frankly—finding someone like that is a rarity.*"

WARREN BUFFETT, 2002, TALKING ABOUT JIM KILTS,
CEO OF GILLETTE[1]

Early in my career, I was working on a large-scale research study with one of the most prestigious international consulting firms. I was the only outside consultant on a team with eight partners and associates, all of whom had graduated from very elite academic institutions.

As an objective observer of this group, I quickly noticed that most of the best thinking and ideas were being generated by one person. Her name was Barbara.* She was the only woman in the group, and while she was not the most aggressive or charismatic person in the room, she consistently saw, with exceptional clarity, what needed to get done and how best to do it.

Because of her less aggressive personality, she was not always credited with contributing the group's best thinking, though even to the most casual observer it was clear she was the source.

Given that Barbara's academic record and work experience were on a par with those of the other members of the team, clearly what she possessed was a distinct type of intelligence, one that couldn't necessarily be identified

*Name changed

on the basis of academic pedigree. After all, her colleagues had graduated from the same prestigious schools. Yet of the eight employees in the room, she was the one to most consistently come up with the best answers.

This observation perplexed me; after all, how, in an institution that prided itself on hiring only the finest minds, could one person's insights so clearly stand out from the rest? I took these questions to my mentor, Michael Scriven, whose distinguished academic career has spanned more than five decades. After I'd spoken excitedly and animatedly, telling him about this mysterious phenomenon I had "discovered," he chuckled and remarked, "just noticed that, did you?"

He went on to explain that this ability has been known about and commented on for decades. He then went into a lengthy critique of the research that had been done on the topic to date. Seeing my disappointment on learning that this amazing "discovery" had already been discovered, he offered a hint of encouragement. "Justin, obviously many people have delved into this topic before," he said. "But there may be room for you to do something new. You'll just have to go in a different direction. You might consider the role that critical thinking and intelligence have in all of this."

And so, I began to study the individual components of critical thinking and intelligence, and their roles in business decision-making. I was surprised to learn that just as Scriven had hinted, very few other researchers had tried to understand how certain aspects of IQ could provide the answer.

# What Every Business Needs

||||||||||||||||||||||||||||

Jim Collins, one of the world's most influential management researchers and commentators, calls them the "right people."[1] Jack Welch, arguably the most successful CEO of the twentieth century, says they're "stars,"[2] while famed author and professor Peter Drucker, pictures them as "masterful conductors."[3] These experts are describing the people who truly determine whether an organization thrives or fails.

But what makes these "star" executives so effective? If we knew, we could identify these traits in others and, more important, develop them within ourselves. The problem is that nobody has accurately identified the fundamental characteristics that make someone a "masterful conductor."

There have been literally hundreds of books and thousands of theorists that have tried to answer this question. At various times we've been told that the secret to management success is the ability to: lead, anticipate change, be entrepreneurial, break all the rules, communicate, be compassionate, compensate for one's weaknesses, foster diversity, express empathy, encourage teamwork, get everyone on the same page, introduce innovation, practice intrapreneurialism, manage logistics, hone marketing expertise, master the value chain, play to one's strengths, put employees first, put employees second (and the customer first), stick to one's knitting, develop subservient leadership, instill values, communicate a vision . . . and that's just a partial list.

nventory, yet it does nothing to illuminate the
result, these theories constitute a costly dis-
t really causes leadership excellence. So, if
our executive ranks with the "right" people
ne one of them ourselves, we need to discover the *es-*
nponents that make someone a "star."

It turns out there are specific cognitive aptitudes that to a large extent determine whether an executive succeeds or fails. And it is these aptitudes that form the foundation of a new theory of intelligence. Not the type of intelligence that determines success in school, but rather the cognitive skills specific to the business environment. We call this new theory Executive Intelligence.

This book

- Introduces the cognitive abilities that top business performers have that make them different from the rest of us

- Critiques how experts have overlooked these critical abilities, flooding the market with methods and theories that are gravely inadequate when it comes to differentiating business talent

- Reveals how Executive Intelligence is measured

- Explains how Executive Intelligence can be taught

Relying upon extensive empirical research as well as exclusive interviews with some of the world's most accomplished business leaders, this book will reveal a new, substantive understanding of "the right stuff"—that which actually differentiates star leaders from everyone else.

# Where Things Went Wrong

||||||||||||||||||||||||

In many ways this book is a condemnation of the world of management science, a world of which I am a part. Management science is a massive industry that is responsible for identifying the best leadership practices, but the field has become overrun by faddish and unproven ideas.

As we will see in this book, researchers have for too long been enamored with attributes, such as personality and style, that are only tangentially related to how well executives actually do their job. For example, while it may be nice for a leader to be very likable or charismatic, these qualities have nothing to do with their ability to get to the "right" answer. Getting to the truth of what is really going on is the primary responsibility of any manager, and the capacity to do so is largely determined by their level of intelligence. Therefore, assessing and cultivating this ability must be made a primary focus of leadership research.

Yet, in our hiring and training practices, we do not pay nearly enough attention to ensuring that we are getting smart people, though there is absolutely no doubt that intelligence is a key determinant of success. We can quibble about what precise percentage of performance it accounts for, but no one can seriously question that smartness—the intellectual ability to do the job—is one of the primary determinants of whether someone succeeds or fails at managerial work.

In fact, even the crude application of IQ tests, which were not even designed to measure business intelligence, remain among the most accurate means of predicting managerial success.

Research has shown that administering a twelve-minute IQ test can predict job performance nearly as well as the best two-hour job interview;[1] so obviously, IQ tests measure something important. This fact has been proven numerous times, with the most recent demonstration being presented in 2004, when two of the most respected researchers in assessment methodologies, Professors Frank Schmidt of the University of Iowa and John Hunter of Michigan State University, published a comprehensive study comparing the predictive power of IQ tests to that of other assessment methodologies. Combining the results of 515 independent studies involving over 100,000 employees, they declared that cognitive ability (IQ) tests predict occupational performance "better than any other ability, trait, or disposition, and better than job experience."[2]

Cognitive ability tests have repeatedly been proven to be a highly effective means for predicting work performance in virtually any profession. Moreover, research has demonstrated that as the complexity of a job increases, so does the predictive validity of these tests. So for managerial positions, considered the most complex of all occupational groups, cognitive-ability measures have been shown to be among the most powerful predictors of success.[3]

Yet nobody has attempted to first determine what makes IQ tests so predictive and then to build upon that understanding as the basis for a theory of business intelligence. Of course, managers need other qualifications. There are thirty-year-olds who score in the genius range on intelligence measures, but it would be irresponsible to make one a CEO of a *Fortune* 500 company just on that basis. Nonetheless, we should never lose sight of the fact that executives do not lead companies with their hands; they lead them with their minds. So without possessing the requisite amount of cognitive ability for the workplace, a leader has little chance for success.

And yet we almost never measure how much intelligence someone has before we either hire or promote them. It is easy to understand why, since to date we have not had a form of cognitive-ability assessment that is acceptable to executives. Though IQ tests are powerfully predictive, these instruments have too many shortcomings to be used with a modern, managerial population.

For instance, it is hard to see the immediate relevance of the typical test question to workplace tasks. A question like "Man is to ape as butterfly is to what?" appears totally unrelated to any decision an executive actually confronts.

Further, many researchers have challenged the accuracy of these traditional intelligence measures by suggesting that the tests themselves are often so biased and flawed—in terms of race, gender, or economic background—that they do not accurately reflect the amount of intelligence that a particular person possesses.[4]

The reservations many hold about the validity of IQ testing for professional assessment have created a situation where IQ is almost never used as a screening tool for executives. What's more, the unfavorable reputation of intelligence testing has inhibited leadership experts from trying to understand the lessons that can be learned from them. This has created a dilemma: businesses are demanding a means to identify and develop star leadership talent, yet they have been provided with no tools to ensure that individuals have the smarts required to excel.

But, instead of correcting the problems with intelligence testing we have gone completely in the other direction. We attempt to use gut feel, personal beliefs about leadership ("she should be charismatic" or "likable"), or emotional intelligence measures to identify the people, who, in Peter Drucker's words, will be "masterful conductors."[5]

The key to solving this problem is to bring the concept of intelligence back into the business arena in an acceptable form. That is what has given life to the notion of Executive Intelligence. Instead of crudely adapting tests that were originally designed to measure the academic potential of schoolchildren, I have sought to develop a new theory of intelligence that is appropriate for a business setting—one that can yield an accurate measure of a manager's relevant cognitive strengths or Achilles' heels.

Executive Intelligence can provide a benchmark that allows a comparison of individuals on the business "smarts" that are essential for performance. Even more important, the theory makes specific the aptitudes that allow some managers to make the "right" move time and time again. Identifying and understanding those fundamental skills provides us with an opportunity to improve them in ourselves and others.

# SECTION I:

# WHAT *IS* EXECUTIVE INTELLIGENCE— AN OVERVIEW

# CHAPTER 1

## Part One: Making the Invisible Visible

In today's workplace, an individual cannot become a star executive without possessing a unique type of business "smarts" that we call Executive Intelligence. Historically, business "smarts" has been a bit like the word "indecency." As Supreme Court Justice Potter Stewart once said when asked to define the latter, "I can't tell you what it is, but I know it when I see it."[1] Still, we have all caught glimpses of this kind of intelligence, even in everyday situations, as the following example illustrates.

A truck was jammed underneath a highway overpass, and the fire department and a tow-truck driver were attempting to free the vehicle. But despite their earnest efforts, the truck remained stubbornly lodged. A motorist, annoyed by the delay, approached the fire chief and asked what the problem was. "The bridge is not high enough," the chief responded impatiently, "so the truck is wedged, and we're having trouble getting it out."

The gentleman responded, "It seems like the problem is that the truck is not low enough to get through." The fire chief laughed. "Yes, I guess that's another way to say it." The motorist persisted, "What I mean is, why don't you make the truck lower by letting the air out of the tires." Ten minutes later the truck was freed from the tunnel and traffic was moving again.

This kind of logic often appears to observers to be as clever as a magic trick—a mysterious act with an impressive outcome. But just seeing the result does not get us any closer to understanding how the feat was accomplished. And if you do not know how the trick was performed, you cannot replicate it or teach it to others.

To create a useful understanding of the concept of business "smarts," we need to pull back the curtain and show how the magic trick is done. What's more, we need a consistent and reliable way to recognize and measure this kind of intelligence if we are to develop it in ourselves and also ensure that decision-making responsibilities are assigned to those best qualified to handle them.

So how do we define Executive Intelligence? In its simplest form, it is a distinct set of aptitudes that an individual must be able to demonstrate in three central contexts of work: the accomplishment of **tasks,** working with and through other **people,** and judging **oneself** and adapting one's behavior accordingly.

On the job, executives are constantly pursuing a variety of goals. They must decide which tasks to accomplish, in what order to do them, and how best to carry them out. They must find ways to meet their goals through the efforts of and cooperation with other people. And always they must actively evaluate themselves, identify their own errors, and make adjustments to correct them.

The more proficient an individual is in all three of these areas, the higher his or her level of Executive Intelligence. Obviously, Executive Intelligence does not consist of a single ability or isolated skill. Rather, it is a blend of critical aptitudes that guide an individual's decision-making process and behavioral path.

Executive Intelligence has its roots in what is commonly known as critical thinking, but it is not the same as the abstract-logic and reasoning skills often associated with that subject. Instead, it is an expanded and applied type of critical thinking; specifically it is how an individual skillfully uses the available information as a guide to thought and action.

This type of intelligence permeates every aspect of managerial work. A close analysis reveals a set of consistent, interrelated skills that form the very foundation of smart executive behavior. In a sense, the theory of Executive Intelligence pulls back the curtain and reveals the magic behind exceptional leadership performance.

We will go into greater detail about the components of the three areas of Executive Intelligence—**tasks, other people, and oneself**—later in the book. But the following examples will give you an idea of the essential role Executive Intelligence plays in business.

# Part Two: Executive Intelligence in Real Life— Accomplishing Tasks

||||||||||||||||||||||||||||

Do you think most senior-level leaders demonstrate the Executive Intelligence required to make good decisions? Think again. When it comes to accomplishing **tasks,** the lack of Executive Intelligence is a pervasive problem in the most senior ranks of corporate America, and it is responsible for some of its most catastrophic business failures. Here's one real-life example:

In the 1980s General Motors was struggling with terrible labor relations. Strikes and the high costs of unionized labor were taking a terrible toll on GM's profitability. At the same time, U.S. manufacturers were losing market share to more efficient Japanese competitors. GM's CEO, Roger Smith, boldly decided to confront this problem head-on. Rather than submit to a long-term erosion of GM's competitive position, he decided to transform the way GM built cars. Smith believed that by making use of the latest robotic technology, he could replace much of the labor force throughout all of GM's plants. He thought this would allow him to address both his labor-relations and his plant-efficiency problems with one elegant solution.

By the end of the 1980s, however, GM had spent more than $45 billion on plant automation—a sum that at the time would have been enough to purchase both Toyota and Nissan—yet more market share had been lost and plant productivity had fallen every year following automation.[2]

How did this seemingly logical solution go so wrong? Roger Smith demonstrated a severe lack of Executive Intelligence in his analysis. First, he failed to consider that while labor is indeed expensive and often problematic, relying upon machines alone may not be less so. In Executive-Intelligence terms, he failed to question his *underlying assumption:* robots equal cheaper cars. Even a quick glance at readily available data would have revealed that machines require huge capital expenses and call for highly skilled support technicians. Second, he failed to anticipate the *unintended consequences* of his initiative: plant automation can severely limit flexibility and the ability to change product lines.

When Robert Lutz, a senior executive in the auto industry, later examined the issue, he determined that the best answer to GM's productivity problems would, in fact, have been a combination of man and machine that maximized the value-added of each.[3]

Now let's look at how another CEO confronted serious challenges to his company's long-term viability.

In 1996, when Keith Grossman was hired as Thoratec Corporation's CEO, the medical-devices company was losing money and struggling to survive. Grossman was charged with helping the company to profitably produce and market their flagship product, a cardiac-assist device. What he quickly realized, however, was that even if he achieved this goal, Thoratec's business model was not sustainable.

As Grossman put it, "The challenge was to turn Thoratec into an enduring company. It was clear that we could get to profitability, but in the context of our industry, we didn't have what it took to sustain."

Without a diversified and integrated product line, Grossman knew it was only a matter of time until Thoratec's market share eroded and its profits were eliminated. He saw only two possibilities for his company's survival—"to acquire or be acquired." At the end of a two-year process to determine in which direction to go, a competitor, Thermo Cardiosystems, was identified as a desirable acquisition. There was just one problem. Thermo Cardiosystems was more than three times the size of Thoratec, and it had a rival product that was doing very well in the market. How, Grossman wondered, was he going to convince his competitor that an acquisition was in both parties' best interest? What's more, how was he going to convince Thermo Cardiosystems to accept Thoratec's stock, management team, and a minority position on Thoratec's board as terms of the deal?

Thermo Cardiosystems's initial attitude toward Thoratec's overtures was skeptical, if not incredulous. But Grossman's presentation to Thermo Cardiosystems' board was unassailable in its logic. He pointed out the existence of large global companies that focus on much more than a single product. As Grossman said, "In this market, there are big companies that don't just work on a single device, they focus on whole diseases. They are combining drugs and devices, and advertising directly to doctors and consumers. They are releasing third- and fourth-generation products. It becomes unrealistic to think that as a small company you are going to be able to just build your way into that market, compete with that, and remain relevant."

Faced with this logic, the Thermo Cardiosystems board began to recognize that they suffered from the same vulnerability as Thoratec, and that rather than seeing each other as competitors, they needed to recognize that the two companies could be much stronger as a single one. They were also very impressed with Grossman's exceptional clarity regarding the fundamental realities of their industry and how best to confront them. Thermo Cardiosystems agreed to the acquisition and Grossman's terms. Today Thoratec is a thriving, highly profitable company with a virtual monopoly in its medical niche.

What did Grossman do that was so impressive? First, he recognized the flaws in his industry's conventional wisdom. Start-up medical-device companies were always so focused on the challenge of taking their product from idea to market that they assumed that success in these areas would automatically result in a viable business. Grossman helped them understand that this *underlying assumption*—successful product necessarily equals successful company—was not sound.

He also pointed out that this model created a very costly *unintended consequence.* Namely, it required the creation of an expensive infrastructure to produce and sell the product. Single-product companies suffered from severe cost handicaps, since they had to create the same infrastructure whether they sold a single device or a hundred different ones. Accordingly, they could never hope to compete with companies offering vast and integrated product lines.

As Grossman said so convincingly to the board:

"This is the model of the future. Someone is going to do it; you're either going to be part of it, or you're going to compete with it. Someone is going to come along with a meaningful presence, a variety of options, and a lot of salespeople in the field. It might as well be us."

This kind of intelligence represents the cornerstone of effective leadership. Grossman's argument was neither propaganda nor brainwashing. And it certainly wasn't a threat. Instead his articulation of facts and conclusions was so sound in its logic that others willingly adopted them as their own.

Executive Intelligence is central to leadership performance because it helps executives articulate considerations that move others, in their own interest, to agree with a decision. It simply enables them to understand the "rightness" of a decision or action. This is an essential and effective means of persuasion because it does not deny anyone's right to make up his or her mind.[4] Assuming that you have put forward a sound argument, others will come to agree with you and thereby adopt your viewpoint as their own.

This method of guiding and persuading others is how executives skillfully turn thinking into action.

## Executive Intelligence in Real Life— Understanding People

The second essential context in which executives must demonstrate intelligence involves working with other **people**. But instead of focusing on an individual's personality, likability, and manners, and calling that a form of intelligence, Executive Intelligence focuses on the specific cognitive skills that allow an individual to understand and navigate the complexities of interpersonal situations in an intelligent way. Let's look at a real-life example from the Boeing Company of a CEO fighting to restore his company's profitability, but lacking the Executive Intelligence to do so.

The story of Philip Murray Condit's seven-year tenure as chairman and CEO of the Boeing Company is a tale of a manager promoted beyond his abilities. The skills that had made him a successful engineer—brilliant academic success and technical problem-solving—were of less use in his leadership position. A severe lack of Executive Intelligence, particularly in the area of social awareness, caused him to be repeatedly blindsided by public scandals. Condit was ineffective and isolated as a CEO, unable to read the complex interpersonal politics surrounding him or to respond effectively. His lack of social perceptiveness blinded him to the "ends justifies the means" sales culture that was welling up around him, as senior members of his team became involved in highly questionable dealings—practices that a more aware CEO would have discovered and stopped early on. As a result, a company that had long been a paragon of American industrial excellence ensnared itself in one scandal after another under his watch.

For example, Boeing's CFO Michael Sears negotiated to receive inflated prices from a Pentagon official, Darleen Druyun, in exchange for Druyun's future employment at Boeing.[5] In 2004, Michael Sears pled guilty for his personal role in the scandal, and was sentenced to several months in federal prison.[6] Further, in 2003, Boeing was banned from bidding on certain Air Force contracts because it improperly obtained and used competitors' information to gain an advantage over rival bids.[7]

Boeing has said that there is no evidence linking Condit to the scandals. But insiders say there were repeated warning signals sent to Condit, which he either mishandled or chose to ignore.

"Condit booked a huge amount of defense business by allowing his subordinates to play business close to the edge," said Loren Thompson, a defense analyst at the Lexington Institute in Arlington, Virginia. The effect on the bottom line was that in 2003 alone, Boeing took more than $1 billion in deal-related write-offs. And the scandals ultimately forced Condit to resign in November of 2003.[8]

How did Condit go so wrong? His failure to recognize how far some of his employees might be willing to go to procure contracts demonstrated a severe lack of Executive Intelligence regarding people. Specifically, he never understood that the *underlying agendas* of some of his executives could easily put them in direct and repeated conflict with ethical business practices. Condit's decision to allow his people to police themselves, without clear oversight, demonstrated a lack of interpersonal awareness that cost Boeing enormously. Further, he never *appropriately considered the probable effects* of his actions. By failing to rein in his subordinates' activities, despite warnings from some of his staff, Condit underestimated how short-term financial gains could be eclipsed by the massive costs—in money and reputation—that these practices would incur.

Let's consider how another CEO confronted a complex interpersonal situation that threatened his company's ability to survive.

Van Johnson tells of a watershed moment in his tenure as CEO of Sutter Health, one of the nation's leading health-care networks, providing services to more than one hundred different communities. One of Sutter's largest payers, Blue Cross, was the source of many difficulties that threatened to bankrupt Sutter's hospitals and physician groups. It was a crucial but delicate issue.

"Virtually everyone at Sutter was having a problem with this particular payer. We weren't getting paid, or we weren't getting paid on time. And what we *were* getting paid was way below what everybody else in the market was getting."

Johnson was faced with a dilemma: take on Blue Cross in a battle that would risk having his hospitals and physician groups removed from Blue Cross's list of providers, or sit back and watch much of his network sink into bankruptcy. Unfortunately, other providers that had taken aggressive stances and gotten into protracted battles with insurers had not fared very well. In fact, for a number of them it had led to a total collapse of their health-care system. Johnson feared the same fate for Sutter.

However, everyone in Sutter was screaming for a fight. The staff saw Blue Cross as an evil and greedy corporation, bent on squeezing out profits even if it meant forcing community medical-care groups into insolvency.

But Johnson saw the situation differently. He recognized that "taking the fight" to Blue Cross was likely to erupt in a costly battle that would hurt everyone involved. He knew he had to find an alternative, and that the first step would be to better understand Blue Cross's perspective.

To that end, he called Dan Crowley, former CEO of Foundation Health, another insurance payer that Johnson had done business with in the past. Over lunch, he and Crowley discussed the situation from an insurer's point of view.

"Dan looked at things from the eyes of a health plan. The business for a health plan is very different from our business. You'd think they were similar, but their motivations are very different. He helped me understand how. I had to find someone outside my own business that understood it. He had been CEO of an insurer, and he knew their perspective."

Standing in Blue Cross's shoes helped Johnson see the problem in an entirely new light, and it opened up an alternative path to resolving the conflict. He studied Blue Cross's administrative systems and tried to understand the ways that the insurer's procedures were failing to meet Sutter's needs. But he also took a look at Sutter's own systems, to see how they were contributing to Blue Cross's difficulties.

"I really had to make sure I understood the case. What's wrong with their billing process? Why does it take them so long to pay? What could I offer to Blue Cross that would assist them? I couldn't just go to them and say fix it without any specifics about how our two systems could work better together.

I then sat down with Ron Williams of Blue Cross, now with Aetna, and we were able to talk about the fundamental issues. But it wasn't about fighting with him, or saying Sutter isn't going to take this anymore. It was about trying to find common ground.

And that's where Ron Williams and I spent the most time. How were we [Sutter] making problems for Blue Cross and how were they making problems for us. Of course it [the discussion] was also about rates. But it had more to do with how do we deal with each other and could improve our processes together. It was a two-way deal. And frankly we [Sutter] had some problems that couldn't be changed overnight. We had to get some consolidation and business practices standardized that were causing a lot of our problems with Blue Cross."

By approaching the situation with a fuller understanding of Blue Cross's perspective, Johnson was able to take a much more constructive approach to the negotiations. Though, ultimately, Sutter and Blue Cross were at odds for approximately three months, the two parties were able to resolve their differences and create a much better long-term relationship.

"You can't just assume someone out there is a bad guy. You create as many problems for them as they do for you. You better figure out what role you have in the problem, take responsibility for that, and offer to change, if you are going to turn around and expect them to change for you.

This approach established a different tone to our dialogue. It wasn't about egos or power struggles. It was about what was fair and bringing the system more into balance."

Johnson's approach to these negotiations yielded impressive results for Sutter. The new terms and the standardization processes that they implemented have allowed Sutter to avoid any cost increases for more than six years following these talks.

"Today Blue Cross is one of our most fair payers. They pay on time. They fixed some of their internal procedures. We addressed our own internal issues that also needed to change. Not that everyone is happy, but it's much fairer now. It brought things into balance."

How did Van Johnson bring about such a favorable outcome to a seemingly unwinnable situation? First, he recognized the *probable effects* of a fight with Blue Cross. Such an approach would be so costly that it would likely spell doom for Sutter. Johnson knew he had to find an alternative. By enlisting the help of Dan Crowley, a CEO of another insurance company, he was able to better understand the *likely underlying agendas* of Blue Cross. And by viewing the situation from Blue Cross's perspective, he was able to skillfully construct an approach much more likely to yield a successful result.

## Executive Intelligence in Real Life— Judging Oneself

Executive Intelligence is also essential when it comes to assessing oneself and correcting one's own errors, as the following example shows.

Wolfgang Schmitt was Rubbermaid's CEO when it was named *Fortune* magazine's "Most Admired Company" in 1993. Just five short years later the company was in such bad shape it was acquired by turnaround specialists, the Newell Corporation. What went wrong? During the 1990s Rubbermaid's market changed dramatically, as retailers began focusing on lower cost over innovation. But Schmitt refused to respond to these market pressures. He was quoted as saying, "In the past we have always had a good history of implementing price increases. We must focus on making sure the customer understands the necessity of these price increases." [9]

When his executives and salespeople repeatedly pointed out the fundamental changes in the market, and the need for Rubbermaid to cut their prices in order to remain competitive, Schmitt refused to listen. Even when Rubbermaid's largest customer, Walmart, warned Schmitt that they would not accept Rubbermaid's price increases, Schmitt chose to stand his ground. Walmart responded by giving much of Rubbermaid's shelf space to lower-priced competitors. [10]

Wolfgang Schmitt suffered from a severe lack of Executive Intelligence about himself; specifically he failed to *encourage and use information that revealed an error in his own judgment*. In today's fast-paced environment, leaders constantly have to make on-the-spot decisions with limited information. Even the sharpest executive makes frequent mistakes, and oversights are sometimes unavoidable. While nobody can expect managers to get it right every time, what is important is that they actively seek out and welcome information that identifies the flaws in their own thinking or actions.

Schmitt's inability to *look critically at his own biases or limitations in perspective* caused him to devalue the essential information that those around him were trying to provide. Because superior action-planning requires the use of multiple perspectives, leaders who lack Executive Intelligence about themselves—those who resist suggestions that force them to reconsider their own thinking—will never reach the best decisions.

Effective executive action always calls for an individual to be able to turn a critical eye on his or her own thinking and behavior. Whether in a strategy-planning meeting, a one-on-one exchange, or any other business format, a leader must be able to test the limits of his or her own ideas against those of others. This is not to suggest that skilled executives are robots who do not feel emotions such as defensiveness, but rather that they can recognize their own mistakes without being blinded by their reactions to them.

Consider how another CEO more skillfully addressed his own significant oversight and acted quickly to minimize its costs to his organization.

In his twenty-five-year tenure with Cedars-Sinai Medical Center, Tom Priselac had made a special effort to establish and maintain personal relationships with the managers and staff throughout the hospital. "My closeness to the organization had served me well, in that people were comfortable in giving me information."

But in late 2002, as Cedars' CEO, Priselac confronted a situation that opened his eyes to a troubling reality; he was in actuality quite out of touch with many of the people in his organization. This was reflected in a union effort to organize the hospital's nurses. The union recruiters had taken advantage of a growing animosity and a lack of trust between the nursing staff and the administration. For instance, there was a tremendous amount of concern among the nurses about their retirement plan. The administration was taking steps to improve the plan, but the antagonism was such that people did not believe the administration would do the right thing.

This lack of trust was particularly distressing to Priselac, a CEO who prided himself on being connected with both managers and employees. He began an aggressive organization-wide initiative called "Lessons Learned" to figure out how the executive team, managers, and staff had grown so far apart, and what needed to be done to repair the problem. Priselac also insisted that the effort focus on how his own actions had allowed this rift to occur despite what he thought were his best efforts to the contrary. With the help of the medical center's organizational-development staff and personal conversations, Priselac came to terms with his role in the crisis.

How could he have missed this serious problem? "Well, we all get into comfort zones. If you asked me before, 'Am I in touch with our managers and employees?' the answer was 'yes.' But when I reflected on it further, I realized that I wasn't having quality contacts with those I already knew and over the years many new people had come into the organization with whom I had not had the opportunity to establish a rapport. It wasn't the broad-based contact I needed."

Although Priselac had made an effort to stay connected with his colleagues and staff during his twenty-five-plus years at Cedars, he realized that he had not worked to maintain the quality of relationships with people he had known for a long time. Compounding this was Cedars' attrition rate of 5 to 10 percent per year, and Priselac's failure to recognize that his organization was increasingly populated by people who did not know him. And he had no system in place to address this.

"It wasn't a conscious thing." Quite to the contrary, he had long utilized employee-satisfaction surveys and followed traditional best practices for tracking employee attitudes. "A lot of the objective measures looked fine. We were growing. Employee satisfaction looked reasonable in some aspects and showed potential for improvement in others, but in the aggregate it didn't show (or, better said, I didn't see) the depth of the problem. The red flags looked yellow, not red."

In retrospect, though, Priselac acknowledged "that people did not know me. I began to lose the value of the frankness these connections gave me." In discussions with board leaders, his colleagues, managers, and employees, he took responsibility for his mistakes that had led to the problem.

Priselac then set about aggressively correcting his behavior. "I changed the way I am visible in the organization, meeting privately and with small groups of directors, managers, and employees (both old and new) in a much more frequent and focused way. The purpose was to create the right kind of venue to have the right kind of contact with people. By doing this on a regular basis, a continuing dialogue has developed, and it has created a more effective feedback loop."

Today, approximately 85 percent of Cedars-Sinai's 8,000 employees who responded on the employee survey rated top management as fair, honest, and trustworthy, and 92 percent would recommend the organization as an employer. These statistics represent a 30 percent increase in employee satisfaction from 2002, when the labor relations troubles peaked. In late 2004, the union that had been attempting to represent the nurses completely withdrew their petition. How did Priselac engineer such an impressive turnaround in such a short period of time?

His exceptional Executive Intelligence about himself was an essential factor. He actively *encouraged and used information that revealed errors in his own judgment.* In undertaking the "Lessons Learned" initiative, he asked that the analysis start with an intense focus on his own role in the breach with employees. Further, he looked *critically at limitations in his own perspective,* namely how over time he had unintentionally become isolated. Priselac's earnest effort to understand his own role in the problem reflected his willingness to make rapid changes that would correct the situation as soon as possible.

# Part Three:
# Executive Intelligence
# Explains Business Smarts

||||||||||||||||||||||||||

The preceding examples show noteworthy executive successes and failures. But while reading about individuals doing their jobs poorly or well might be interesting, it is much more useful to discover what it is that these successful individuals have in common. It is through that analysis that a pattern can be discerned and useful insights gained.

Each of the recounted stories involved executives facing entirely different problems. But regardless of the topic, the successful leaders arrived at their solution through the effective application of certain cognitive skills. This is the common thread that we have been searching for. And once we realize that there is a commonality in the way that exceptional executives approach and solve problems, we move one step closer to identifying what it is that is woven into the inner fabric of these people.

What we are seeking is an understanding of the underlying wellspring of these faculties. However, this recognition will not yield a step-by-step decision-making guide. Business schools and managerial training often provide useful models that can help people make sound decisions. But just as the best surgical instruments are unlikely to be effective in unskilled hands, even the best problem-solving paradigms require *intelli-*

*gence* at each step in the model. By exploring and defining this intelligence, we can better identify it in others and cultivate it in ourselves.

What we are talking about is an internalized set of skills, those that finally make explicit the elusive concept of "business acumen." The demands of today's corporate environment have made Executive Intelligence a decisive factor in becoming a star in business. These cognitive abilities represent the essential human capital advantage that today's corporations desperately need.

Patricia "Pat" Russo, the CEO responsible for the impressive turnaround of Lucent Technologies, has experienced firsthand what a difference such people make in your business.

"It's a real challenge to find people that have the ability to take a great deal of information and separate it into what matters and what doesn't matter. Many people tend to get lost or defocused when addressing a complex issue, but it's the people who have what I call "clarity of thought" that really make the difference. I'm often asked during a talent search what I'm looking for, and my response always includes 'clear thinkers.' There are clear thinkers, muddled thinkers, and people that fall in between. Clear thinkers—the ones that can cull everything down into the right point—can be very hard to find. But if you get yourself a team of clear thinkers, the possibilities are endless.

These are the high-value executives I am always seeking. They are good listeners and are thoughtful, and they apply those traits to any set of issues with which they are engaged. They have the ability to listen openly, reflect on varying viewpoints, and rapidly synthesize what is useful or meaningful when dealing with a particular issue. They quickly get to the core of a problem."

In addition to describing the skills that these people have, Russo is explaining their value to an organization, and how hard they are to find. These "stars" are, in fact, what allows businesses to race ahead of their competition.

Robert Johnson, the founder, chairman, and CEO of Black Entertainment Television (BET), and one of the world's most successful entrepreneurs, explains further:

> "Even the sharpest thinkers need teams of sharp people around them. And these high-performing teams develop over time. It is one of the basic laws of attracting talent: the more talented people you have, the more talented people you can attract. You get the highest level of input in decision-making and the best critique of things you should or should not undertake when you are surrounded by such individuals. Once you reach that critical mass of talent, there's literally nothing you can't undertake."

As Russo and Johnson point out, the success of any business depends upon assembling a group of exceptionally sharp people. Yet, traditional business training does not ensure that an individual will have these capabilities. As any experienced CEO will attest, merely graduating from a top business school does not guarantee that a person will become a skilled executive. In order to consistently identify and cultivate the talent that is needed, the first step must be to define the fundamental skills that make someone a "clear thinker."

# CHAPTER 1 SUMMARY

||||||||||||||||||||||||

- IQ tests have been proven to predict managerial performance, yet because of their shortcomings, these measures have been abandoned as a means for evaluating managerial talent.

- Executive Intelligence is a distinct set of aptitudes that determine one's success in the three central contexts of work: the accomplishment of **tasks,** working with and through other **people,** and assessing/adapting **oneself.**

- Executive Intelligence consists of a set of consistent, interrelated skills that forms the foundation of smart executive behavior and affects every aspect of professional decision-making.

- Lack of Executive Intelligence is a pervasive problem in the most senior ranks of corporate America, and it is responsible for some of the most catastrophic business failures.

- Star leaders possess high Executive Intelligence, which in large part determines why they are so successful.

- Assembling teams of "clear thinkers," those with high executive intelligence, is essential for organizational success.

# CHAPTER 2

# Part One:
# Critical Thinking—
# The Foundation of
# Executive Intelligence

|||||||||||||||||||||||

After studying leadership for more than thirty years, Professor Henry Mintzberg of McGill University, the author of such landmark studies as *The Nature of Managerial Work,* began to question the importance of business school training. "I ask people who know American business well to name three or four chief executives who really made a difference," Mintzberg said, "not short-term, but who really sustained superb performance. Almost never does anybody mention a Harvard MBA, let alone any MBA."[1]

Andrea Jung, the CEO of Avon, has made a similar observation:

"Clear thinking in senior leadership is a primary attribute we look for: at Avon we even test for it. I've seen little correlation between those that have received a formal business education and those that possess clear thinking. Some of our best ideas and thinking have been generated by people with the least formal training. It comes down to the fact that there are some people that have a knack for this and some that don't. And a business education is not the determining factor."

Quinn Spitzer and Ron Evans, of Kepner-Tregoe, an international management-consulting firm, also noted this pattern in their research regarding the world's most successful leaders. How, they asked in their national best-seller, *Heads You Win,* could Sam Walton build WalMart without an MBA, Jack Welch make GE into the most admired company in the world without ever going to business school, and David Packard make HP an industry leader without "business process reengineering"?[2] None of those men had the formal training that is meant to ensure business success. So, could there be something more fundamental to performance than the theories taught in business schools and management books? Spitzer and Evans identified that there was, in fact, a basic determinant of executive success that was totally distinct from the knowledge gained in a business education: an intellectual capacity that they called "critical thinking."

They discovered that the great executives throughout recent history were not just people of action, but also people capable of thought—*critical thought.* With the precision of hindsight, Spitzer and Evans concluded that the critical thinking that leaders such as Jack Welch, Sam Walton, and David Packard brought to bear in their businesses was fundamentally more effective than that of their colleagues and competitors. Their superior thought processes enabled them to better assess complex economic environments and identify appropriate responses to central business issues. When problems arose, they could accurately identify the causes and quickly take corrective action. They made good decisions, balancing the benefits and risks associated with their choices. And they implemented their chosen course of action effectively by circumventing problems and seizing opportunities.[3]

Jack Welch expressed similar views in an interview for this book.

"I don't care if an executive went to a top business school. That doesn't matter to me. It's more about a way of thinking, something I call a 'healthy skepticism.' There's no question that great leaders are constantly looking around corners, anticipating and 'smelling out' issues. For instance, when a deal came to me, I always approached it with the premise that the price was too high, or that it didn't fit with our business. I'd then probe to try to see and prove why it fit, what was good about it, and how it would change us for the better. It's about smelling out what's really going on. Asking the right questions and anticipating problems is a big aspect of leadership. What we are talking about is the granular stuff of business. A leader must have that."

What Welch refers to as the "granular stuff of business" is, in fact, critical thinking. The skills he describes, such as probing, proving, asking the right questions, anticipating problems, are the specific cognitive skills that make up the critical thinking Spitzer and Evans were referring to.

Irene Rosenfeld, CEO of Frito-Lay Inc., explains further:

"The reality is that the gut-feel, the sniffer, knowing what is really going on and what needs to happen, isn't necessarily taught in business school. And for senior executives, needing to see a situation for what it really is comes up all the time.

For instance, I recently had a difficult customer situation that had a lot of people around here very worried. Our customer had asked for some things that, on the face of it, we would have to say no to. But because we always take our customers' concerns seriously, I felt it was important to understand the 'spirit' of what they were asking for rather than just the 'letter.'

Through deeper discussions with the customer, it became clear what they were really concerned about. Once I understood the root cause of their problem, we were able to develop a couple of alternative solutions that were actually quite different from their initial request,

but still addressed the real problem that they were having. And knowing how to do this is not something you necessarily pick up in school."

Rosenfeld's story highlights the complex nature of sizing up a situation
and coming up with a well-crafted solution. She explains that though
these skills are not necessarily gained from even the best business-school
training, they are nonetheless critical to executive success, since these
types of issues are constantly confronted by senior executives. Resolving
such issues is a crucial part of their substantive responsibilities.

Spitzer and Evans more precisely discovered that it was an executive's
capacity for critical thinking that determined how well he or she executed
these essential tasks. They concluded that while executives may hold degrees from the most prestigious business schools, be experienced practitioners of the most celebrated management theories, and receive advice
from respected consultants, it was their aptitude for critical thinking that
determined whether leaders would succeed or fail. The researchers' findings suggest that critical thinking is indeed the stuff that makes intelligent
executive behavior possible.

# Part Two: Critical Thinking Applied to Business

||||||||||||||||||||||||

So what is critical thinking, and how does it determine an executive's effectiveness? Although Spitzer and Evans identified critical thinking as the essential mental ability behind business success, they offered no detailed description or explanation of how it occurs. In order to make their abstract concept more concrete, we need a working definition of critical thinking and a better understanding of its role in business.

Traditionally, critical thinking has been associated with exercises involving simple logic games. A typical question might be: All mallards are ducks, and all ducks fly, therefore all mallards can *"what"* (a: quack; b: swim; c: eat; d: fly). But how is this abstract exercise relevant to business decision-making? It could not possibly constitute the applied critical thinking that Spitzer and Evans discovered as the key to executive success. There must be a definition of critical thinking that is more relevant to business.

Professor Michael Scriven, a former Whitehead Fellow at Harvard University, a professor of psychology at the University of California–Berkeley, and one of the most published authors in this area of research, offered a definition of critical thinking that suggests its essential business role. He described critical thinking as:

The skilled, active interpretation and evaluation of observations, communications, information, and argumentation as a guide to thought
and action.[4]

In other words, critical-thinking ability determines how skillfully someone gathers, processes, and applies information in order to identify the
best way to reach a particular goal or navigate a complex situation. A
basic example of this might be how the manufacturers of the Segway
Human Transporter *could* have analyzed their product's market potential.
The upright powered vehicle was heralded by its makers as a revolution
in human mobility. Despite its impressive hype, however, the Transporter
has been met with a lukewarm reception from consumers and has not
transformed urban transportation as its inventors touted it would.[5]

Using critical thinking, a simplified analysis of Segway's business
plan might look something like this:

For a number of years a mode of transportation has existed that is
functionally similar to the Segway, namely the powered scooter. These
scooters sell for a fraction of the cost of a Segway, yet they have not
been widely adopted, and cities have not altered their infrastructures
to accommodate this mode of transportation.

Why would the Segway succeed where the scooter has failed? The
Segway has two advantages over the scooter: the user can (1) stand and
balance completely upright while moving or stopped, and (2) go backward. The basic question remains, though. Is it the lack of these two
features that kept the scooter from being more widely adopted? If not,
there is little reason to anticipate any greater demand for Segway's
product than for scooters. In fact, because of Segway's dramatically
higher cost, there may be less demand.

This type of thinking—the skillful use of information to reach a conclusion—represents the foundation of sound business decision-making. As Jack Welch noted:

> "Great leaders share a lack of naiveté. There's a rigor in their thinking. A questioning. You need to build self-confidence in people while at the same time challenging the hell out of their assumptions."

In its simplest form, critical thinking in business involves skillfully working out the best answer you can come up with by identifying and using all information that has value for that purpose and resisting irrelevant or unreliable considerations, however tempting they may be.[6] This is not easy, but then again, there are no shortcuts to finding the optimal way to handle a particular situation. Critical thinking is the best guide we have for discovering the "right answers" when it comes to accomplishing tasks, dealing with people, or evaluating and adapting our own behavior.

Recognizing that there is a type of critical thinking that is directly relevant to business has made possible the discovery of Executive Intelligence, which refers to one's capacity for critical thinking in all aspects of executive work. Because of their superior critical thinking, star executives arrive at the right answers more often than their peers. But what is the magic behind their success? Is there some secret formula? Theorists and business professors have tried for years to answer that question, touting their work as "the" guide to sound decision-making. But the truth is there is no magic formula. This is exactly why so many MBAs trained in the best decision-making paradigms fail in the real world. The secret behind a star's success lies in their ability to create a solution tailored to suit each situation at hand.

It's the ephemeral, constantly evolving nature of this process that makes schematic descriptions or step-by-step decision-making guides inadequate. Those tools are only effective to the degree that they are intelligently applied. Critical thinking simply cannot be diagrammed in black and white. Whereas decision-making guides require one to force a given situation to fit a particular model, star thinkers are capable of adapting their analysis to fit any situation.

Rick Lenny, the chairman, president, and CEO of the Hershey Company, who has been widely credited for that corporation's impressive turnaround, explains:

> "I think something is forcing us to be too formulaic. There's a want to make everything simple and put it in a matrix. There's this desire to follow models rather than think. It's how many executives have been taught to do their jobs, and it's tough to get them to act differently."

But, perhaps the best way to understand the thinking processes of star performers is to compare them to ancient scientists, alchemists, who sought to transform base metals into gold. When confronted with a decision, star executives—essentially modern-day alchemists—start with the same base metals as their peers. However, they mix these basic ingredients in a superior way, leading to consistently better results. By customizing their analysis to suit the particular situation, stars yield decision-making gold.

The key to their success actually lies in the means by which they reach a conclusion, rather than in the final conclusion itself. If you dissect an exceptional executive's decision-making process, his or her superior cognitive skills become obvious. For instance, these leaders consistently ask perceptive questions that identify core issues. They discriminate among different sources of data and disregard the less reliable ones. As you trace their thinking to see how they arrived at successful answers, these mental actions are revealed as crucial. But no single activity, or even sequence of activities, can be pointed to as a map for others to follow. At different phases in the analysis, different activities take center stage. The process is shaped by the circumstances, and the solutions the executives identify are uniquely tailored to address each situation.

These people have what some would call an uncanny sense of direction. Not a geographic one, but rather a highly developed intuition for the *analytic* path that will get them to their destination. To an outside observer, the sequence of steps followed in their decision-making process seems hard to pin down. And, indeed, it is a fluid, elastic procedure that changes to suit whatever problem they confront. This is why it has been so difficult to understand or replicate.

The key is to stop looking for paradigms to solve business problems and recognize the inescapably organic nature of on-the-job decision-making. It is an individual's aptitude for critical thinking in business that determines the quality of the approach and of the results, not his or her training in the latest, best-practice problem-solving techniques.

In reality, business critical-thinking is a form of intelligence—an organic, adaptive, ever-evolving set of cognitive skills applied in the business arena. It is what we call Executive Intelligence. But until now, the cognitive skills that make up Executive Intelligence have not been identified or fully understood.

# CHAPTER 2 SUMMARY

||||||||||||||||||||||||||||

- The foundation of Executive Intelligence, critical thinking, has been identified by academic researchers and business leaders alike as being central to success.

- Critical thinking determines how skillfully someone gathers, processes, and applies information in order to identify the best way to reach a particular goal or navigate a complex situation.

- Critical thinking is the best guide we have for discovering the "right answers," because it allows one to identify and use all information that has value for that purpose and to resist irrelevant or unreliable considerations, however tempting they may be.

- Schematic descriptions or step-by-step decision-making guides are inadequate because the secret behind a star's success lies in his or her ability to create a solution tailored to suit each situation that arises.

# CHAPTER 3

## Part One: Discovering Executive Intelligence

|||||||||||||||||||||||

When Alfred Binet was commissioned one hundred years ago to create a measure of academic intelligence, he first identified the school subjects that students needed to learn, such as arithmetic or language skills.[1] Then he set about identifying the specific cognitive skills that determined a student's aptitude for mastering each of these subjects. His work formed the basis for what today is known as the IQ test. Still recognized as the standard for measuring academic intelligence around the world, the test remains the most powerful predictor of a child's academic potential. But while we readily accept that there is a set of cognitive skills that constitute academic intelligence, until now we have labored under the mistaken notion that there is no such thing as intelligence unique to executive skill. In other words, unlike in the case of academic success, we have assumed that no distinctive set of cognitive skills determines business or leadership aptitude.

Yet the work of Quinn Spitzer, Ron Evans, and Michael Scriven suggested that a defined set of cognitive skills did indeed exist. So clearly, what was needed was a test that could isolate these skills. Following Binet's lead, I set about creating a measure of leadership intelligence, one that would be as predictive of leadership performance as Binet's IQ measure was of academic intelligence. The first step was to identify the "subjects," or contexts, of executive work.

Professor Robert Sternberg of Yale University, president of the American Psychological Association and author of *Practical Intelligence in Everyday Life,* outlined the essential work contexts in which managers must perform. Sternberg and his colleagues determined these to be: handling tasks, working with and through other people, and assessing/adapting oneself.[2] These three broad categories cover the totality of executive work, and even a cursory look at what managers do on a daily basis reveals their all-encompassing nature.

Almost every day all business leaders are faced with decisions relating to:

- **Tasks**—managers must formulate strategy, oversee logistics, provide direction, propose new initiatives, and execute plans.

- **People**—executives are required to anticipate and manage conflicts, oversee and manage teams and subordinates, communicate and work well with superiors, and deal with customers.

- **Onself**—leaders must integrate the suggestions or criticisms of others, recognize changing circumstances, and adapt accordingly.

The next step in developing a measure of leadership intelligence relied upon the findings of the most respected minds in management science. From these findings were pulled together a list of the specific cognitive skills that were independently cited as essential to effective leadership. These skills had each been noted separately in business and management-science literature as being common to top performers. Though the compilation of skills was very expansive, there existed overlap, so it was necessary to identify the core aptitudes common to the group, and

then sort these skills into the three categories of [...]
fied by Sternberg. Interestingly, all of the skills [...]
subject categories, and this confirmed the initial p[...]
basic subjects, or contexts, of executive work were an accu[...]
tation of real-world leadership.

By distinguishing the subjects that managers must master and the[...]
pinpointing the cognitive skills that determine an individual's aptitude in
each subject, a theory of leadership intelligence had emerged. Validation
of this theory was accomplished by evaluating real executives for the cognitive skills of interest. A pattern became obvious: star executives consistently outperformed their peers in employing these cognitive skills. What
is more, all of these aptitudes were found to be interdependent and necessary for effective leadership decision-making.

A full list of the cognitive skills, classified by work-subject category,
can be found in the table on the following page.

This list makes explicit the cognitive skills that underpin smart executive behavior. For instance, while we frequently hear how essential it is
for someone to think "outside the box," what actually determines one's
ability to do so? In other words, what skills make someone a creative
thinker? Typically, creative thinkers can view the same issue from *multiple
perspectives*. They are able to *define a particular problem* in several different ways, *anticipate likely obstacles,* and *identify sensible options* for over-
coming those obstacles. Someone's aptitude for these skills determines
how well he or she will perform as a creative thinker.

Or, we often say that someone has exceptional political or social
savvy, but what exactly does that mean? What specific cognitive skills
allow these people to handle interpersonal situations so effectively? Typically, socially skilled people are exceptional at *recognizing underlying
agendas*, gauging how these *agendas may conflict* with one another, and

# IVIDUAL SKILLS THAT COMPRISE
# ECUTIVE INTELLIGENCE

| Regarding Tasks, Great Leaders:[3] | Regarding People, Great Leaders:[4] | Regarding Oneself, Great Leaders:[5] |
|---|---|---|
| Appropriately define a problem and differentiate essential objectives from less relevant concerns. | Recognize the conclusions that can and cannot be drawn from a particular exchange. | Pursue and encourage feedback that may reveal an error in judgment and then make appropriate adjustments. |
| Anticipate likely obstacles to achieving objectives and identify sensible means to circumvent them. | Recognize the likely underlying agendas and motivations of individuals and groups that are involved in a situation. | Demonstrate an ability to recognize one's own personal biases or limitations in perspective, and use this understanding to improve one's own thinking and plans for action. |
| Critically examine the accuracy of the underlying assumptions being relied on. | Anticipate the likely emotional reactions of individuals to actions or communications. | Recognize when serious flaws in one's own ideas or actions require swift public acknowledgment of the mistake and a dramatic change in direction. |
| Articulate the strengths and weaknesses of the suggestions or arguments posed by others. | Accurately identify the core issues and perspectives that are central to a conflict. | Appropriately articulate the essential flaws in the arguments of others, and reiterate the strengths of one's own position. |
| Recognize what is known about an issue, what more needs to be known, and how best to obtain the relevant and accurate information needed. | Appropriately consider the probable effects and likely unintended consequences that may result from taking a particular course of action. | Recognize when it is appropriate to resist the objections of others and remain committed to a sound course of action. |
| Use multiple perspectives to identify likely unintended consequences of various action-plans. | Recognize and balance the different needs of all relevant stakeholders. | |

*anticipating the probable effects and likely unintended consequences* of a chosen course of action. They understand *how those involved will likely react,* and they weight this information appropriately in their response. These specific capabilities determine one's "people smarts."

Nearly everyone acknowledges that executives must be able to recognize their own mistakes and minimize the costs of their missteps. But what allows someone to be "self-aware" and adaptive? Generally such people are highly sensitive to the cues that suggest that they are making a mistake. They *seek out and encourage* this constructive criticism and *use it to make appropriate adjustments* to their plans of action. When they blunder, *they are quick to see their mistake and change course to correct the problem.* People who do these things well are "smart" about themselves.

To better understand how all of the cognitive skills are interrelated, it is useful to revisit Michael Scriven's definition of critical thinking, the foundation upon which the theory of Executive Intelligence is based:

> The skilled, active interpretation and evaluation of observations, communications, information, and argumentation as a guide to thought and action.[6]

In studying the cognitive skills chart as a whole, one fact becomes inescapable. *All* of these cognitive skills that have been cited by management experts as crucial to executive performance have something in common— they all determine how well someone gathers, processes, and applies information in order to identify the best way to reach a particular goal or navigate a complex situation. In other words, these are the skills that allow someone to achieve the highest level of critical thought described by Scriven. It is the combination of these individual skills that allows leadership critical-thinking to occur. And it was this observation that validated the notion that critical thinking was the foundation of leadership intelligence.

Though most executives possess strong skills in one or two of the subject categories (**tasks, other people, and oneself**), it is exceptional ability in all three that constitutes a star. For instance, some individuals can understand and navigate complex interpersonal situations but are hopeless when it comes to analyzing a new strategic initiative. Others might have tremendous analytic skills, but when it comes to dealing with other people, they say or do blundering things at inopportune moments. Still others are simply blind to their own shortcomings and unable to correct for their own missteps. It is the rare and highest-performing executives, however, who possess a combination of skills that allows them to be successful in *all* of these essential areas of executive performance. It is this blend of aptitudes that enables them to consistently outperform their peers.

Pat Russo, CEO of Lucent Technologies, explains:

> "Great leaders have a number of abilities that all must work together in order to accomplish the complex job of a CEO. At one moment you may be using analytics, culling and pressing to get useful information to develop your strategy. In the next moment you may be using your interpersonal skills to effectively motivate and guide your people. So you are constantly switching hats.
>
> It's also important to be open and honest with your team. This lets people know that you are in the boat with them, that you are interested in the truth, and that when they tell you the truth, you would never take it out on them even if it's not exactly what you wanted to hear.
>
> To be good at all these things is rare, but they are critical contributors to great leadership. I can think of some very talented people that have many of these qualities, but not all. For instance, I know one person in particular that is great with analytics and good at dealing with people, but when it comes to accepting the input of others, he just can't handle it. These types of blind spots are common among even the

most senior executives. I don't know what the exact percentage is, but it's pretty rare to find someone that has a good blend of all the necessary skills."

Russo points out how the complexity of senior managerial responsibilities requires a combination of all of the attributes that compose Executive Intelligence. To be good at only one or two of them is not enough, since they all work interdependently with one another.

Let's take a look at a singular, chilling moment in history, one in which the superb facility in all three areas of Executive Intelligence displayed by a chief executive quite literally saved the world from nuclear annihilation. This heroic performance was John F. Kennedy's handling of the Cuban Missile Crisis.[7]

In 1992 a conference in Havana, Cuba, brought together many of the surviving key players involved in the Cuban missile crisis of October 1962. The purpose of this meeting was to shed some light on those historic events and determine for the first time just how close the United States and the Soviet Union had come to nuclear conflict, and how this crisis was averted. Among those attending the conference were Cuba's president Fidel Castro; General Anatoly Gribkov, the Soviet troop commander in Cuba at the time; and Robert McNamara, the U.S. secretary of defense during the crisis.

By the end of their disclosures, a terrifying realization had emerged: those six days had brought the world closer to total obliteration than anyone had ever thought. Both the Americans and the Russians had been alarmingly inaccurate in their perception of the other side's capability and intentions. For instance, it was learned that the U.S. vastly underestimated Soviet troop strength on the island, believing there to be less than ten thousand troops; in reality there were more than forty thousand. Much more significant was the revelation that *these Soviet troops were actually armed with short- and long-range tactical nuclear missiles*. The

American leadership had believed, perhaps wishfully, that the nuclear warheads were not yet within the operational reach of these men.

But not only did the Soviet troops have nuclear weapons, they also had been given orders to use these weapons against the United States if at any time during an attack they lost communication with Moscow. Robert McNamara nearly fell off his chair when he heard that news. He had been present when the U.S. military's Joint Chiefs of Staff had vehemently argued for Kennedy's go-ahead for an all-out attack on Cuba. Knocking out Russian communications would certainly have been a priority from the start. If Kennedy had followed their advice, it would almost surely have meant the extinction of the human race.

Yet Kennedy was able to convince the Soviets to remove their missiles without a single shot being fired. How did he manage this? He demonstrated a rare aptitude for the cognitive skills that make up Executive Intelligence's three essential categories, and he used these skills to bring about a masterful resolution of the crisis.

When Kennedy first learned of the construction of missile sites in Cuba, he knew he had to act. The Soviets could not be allowed to operate with impunity in America's own backyard. The presence of the missiles could be viewed as a dramatic shift in the balance of power in the Cold War, destabilizing what was generally viewed as an already tense equilibrium. Further, allowing the missiles to be placed in Cuba would severely damage Kennedy's domestic credibility, leaving him vulnerable to the charge of being weak on U.S. defense.

All of these considerations were prominent in Kennedy's mind as he guided his cabinet and Joint Chiefs to a solution, but the president never lost sight of his primary, overriding goal: to ensure that whatever his response, he did not back the two superpowers into a corner, lest one of them would feel compelled to launch a nuclear response.

The Joint Chiefs vigorously insisted that Kennedy launch an immediate, large-scale military invasion. Certain that the U.S. would quickly overwhelm the Cuban defenses and the Soviet troops stationed there, they argued that America had to respond to the Soviet's aggression with a decisive, preemptive strike. When Kennedy expressed concern about the likely Soviet reaction, General Curtis Lemay, the Air Force Chief of Staff, stated that the Soviets would not dare risk a military response of their own. One member of the Joint Chiefs went even further and argued that the U.S. should use nuclear missiles, explaining that the Soviets would unquestionably use theirs if they found themselves in a similar position.

The advice from his generals worried Kennedy greatly, but not simply because he found their logic frighteningly dubious. Placing himself in Soviet premier Nikita Khrushchev's shoes, he knew that Khrushchev undoubtedly had generals making similar demands. Kennedy realized how quickly this could get out of control on either side. He pointed out to his brother Robert Kennedy the bitter irony of his military advisers' reasoning: "If they were wrong about the Soviet response, there would be no one left alive to know it."[8]

At each step of the way, before he took any action, Kennedy first looked at the situation from Khrushchev's perspective. At each point in the crisis he had to make it as easy as possible for Khrushchev to back down while still saving face. He felt confident that Khrushchev was also aware of how perilous the situation had become and was not interested in going to war over Cuba. Using this insight, Kennedy reasoned that Khrushchev would prefer a way out rather than a direct confrontation with the U.S.

Secretary of Defense Robert McNamara offered a more desirable response—a naval embargo around Cuba aimed at stopping Soviet progress on the missile site construction. Kennedy followed his suggestion. The action enabled the U.S. to send the message to the Russians that they were serious about the removal of these weapons, but it did not risk immediate casualties on either side. The president knew that any overt military act could quickly force an elevated, potentially irrational response. Though his generals and certain members of Congress accused him of being derelict in his duties as Commander-in-Chief and claimed that his nonmilitary reaction was putting the whole country in grave peril, Kennedy knew his position was sound and that his critics' thinking was dangerously flawed. He stood his ground.

Kennedy's ability to view the situation from the Soviet perspective allowed him to come up with a brilliant potential solution. For years, much to the concern of the Soviets, the U.S. had maintained missiles in Turkey just over the Russian border. But these missiles had become obsolete, and Turkey was already better protected by nuclear-armed Polaris submarines in the Mediterranean. Over the previous eighteen months President Kennedy had twice requested the removal of the Turkish missiles, but his orders had never been carried out. Kennedy now had a valuable way out of the situation in Cuba.

He sent his brother Robert to meet privately with Soviet ambassador Anatoly Dobrynin. As Kennedy predicted, Dobrynin immediately offered the removal of the Russian missiles in Cuba in exchange for the U.S. removal of the offensive missiles in Turkey. Robert Kennedy told Dobrynin that the U.S. could never agree to any demands under threat, but that the president had long believed the Turkish missiles to no longer be of use. If the Soviets removed their Cuban missiles immediately, within a few months they would find that the U.S. missiles in Turkey had disappeared as well.

Thus Kennedy gave Khrushchev the victory he needed to back out of the Cuban situation: Khrushchev could remove the Cuban missiles and declare victory to his generals, saying that he had successfully gotten the U.S. to back down and remove a longstanding threat to the motherland. Khrushchev quickly accepted Kennedy's offer. Upon hearing about the successful resolution of the crisis, Kennedy left his cabinet with strict final orders; no one was ever to suggest that the U.S. had emerged in any way victorious over its Soviet adversary.[9]

How did Kennedy arrive at such an amazing outcome? The answer lies in the exceptional skill with which he reasoned through the complexities of the situation. Simply put, he displayed a tremendous command of the cognitive skills in all three categories of Executive Intelligence. Kennedy showed a sharp awareness of what he could and could not conclude from the facts presented to him and of the assumptions underlying his advisers' suggestions. He remained highly conscious of the Soviet perspective and their likely reactions. And he carefully considered the substance behind the objections of his critics and knew when to hold his ground. He used his reasoning to guide the country to a sound resolution.

Kennedy performed his feat in 1962, and, obviously, "star" performers have been around a lot longer than that. So why has no one discovered Executive Intelligence until now? The answer is that though these skills have been identified as central to high-level executive performance, no one had ever recognized how they actually weave together into a unique, consistent, and measurable form of leadership intelligence, an Executive IQ—an intelligence focused not on academic exercises but rather on one's aptitude for managerial tasks.

# Part Two: The Broad Reach of Executive Intelligence

||||||||||||||||||||||||||

Executive Intelligence is crucial to decision-making in any position of leadership, not just at the CEO level. It dominates leadership performance across industries in the public and private sectors. But, as with any theory, it is necessary to look to real-life examples to fully comprehend how theory translates into actual behavior.

After the tragic events on September 11, 2001, in New York City, Washington, D.C., and Pennsylvania, the American Red Cross set up the Liberty Fund to collect money for the victims and their families. A massive amount of donations flowed in, totaling more than $564 million. But then a shocking secret was leaked—more than half of the money collected would not be going to the intended recipients. It was being set aside for the Red Cross's administrative costs and future needs.

The Red Cross president at the time, Dr. Bernadine Healy, exacerbated the situation when she testified before Congress and vigorously defended the organization's actions. "The Liberty Fund is a war fund. It has evolved into a war fund," she said. "We must have blood readiness. We must have the ability to help our troops if we go into a ground war. We must have the ability to help the victims of tomorrow." Fund contributors and government regulators reacted with outrage. A highly public congressional investigation was launched.[10]

In allocating the money for purposes other than what its donors intended, the Red Cross leadership showed a troubling inability to anticipate the *likely emotional reactions* of donors and government regulators. Making matters worse, when Dr. Healy was confronted with the reality that she and her organization had terribly misjudged public opinion, she stubbornly rejected the criticism as unfounded. In Executive Intelligence terms, she showed an inability to *recognize when serious flaws in her actions require swift acknowledgment of the mistake and a dramatic change in direction.* As a result of the Red Cross's missteps and Healy's failure to acknowledge and correct them, thousands of contributors called the Red Cross to find out where their money had gone and to demand refunds.

The preceding example illustrates how leadership decisions in any field or industry can be analyzed in terms of the cognitive skills that are at the core of Executive Intelligence. By doing this, the underlying causes of a manager's successes or failures can be more readily understood.

In a very different industry, Billy Beane used his exceptional Executive Intelligence to revolutionize the management of a major league baseball franchise.

Since the 1990s, it had become conventional wisdom that only the big-market teams with massive budgets could compete for a championship. Yet Beane, as general manager for the Oakland A's, put together a winning roster using a budget less than one-third of that of his top American League competitor, the New York Yankees. From 1999 to 2004, the A's amassed the second-best win-loss record in the American League, and in an industry in which many teams consistently lose money, Beane's organization made money or broke even from 1998 to 2004.[11]

Beane refused to follow the nearly one-hundred-year-old convention of valuing players solely in terms of traditional statistics, such as batting average, runs batted in, and home runs. By delving deeper into the statistics to determine how much each player contributed to team success, Beane realized that these traditional metrics overlooked other, more important factors. For instance, he realized that the key contribution of a hitter was his ability to get himself on base or to at least wear down the pitcher and make it easier for his teammates to do so. This led Beane to seek out patient players who could go deep into the count and force pitchers to throw as many pitches as possible. What Beane found was that this skill ultimately helped the entire team by fatiguing the opposing pitcher.[12]

This is just one example of how Beane, now one of the most admired general managers in baseball, transformed his team by looking at traditional practices in an entirely different way. In Executive Intelligence terms, Bean *critically examined the accuracy of common assumptions* about what made players valuable, and his insights allowed Oakland to man its roster with players who worked together as a more effective unit. Equally as important, he allowed the A's to avoid chasing the same talent as the rest of the league and paying top dollar for those coveted players.

Executive Intelligence is the essential internal compass that ultimately determines how skillful an individual's actions will be. This does not mean that star executives do not listen to their instincts or to outside expertise; it's just that they use their Executive Intelligence in deciding when to listen and how much to pay attention. After all, one's own instincts or someone else's opinions may help point the way to the right decision, or they may not. Executive Intelligence is the ultimate guide to knowing the difference. For instance, it demands great skill and sensitivity to recognize when a solution to a problem is **well-supported** as opposed to merely **widely accepted.** It also may take courage, because the truth does not always correspond to what is popular. While Beane's approach was initially met with league-wide skepticism for his departure from conventional wisdom, he did not deviate from his strategy. He recognized the baselessness of the criticisms and remained confident in the soundness of his analysis.

While it is useful to learn from the successes and mistakes of others, Executive Intelligence is not just another template or paradigm that instructs people in the steps needed to make a decision. It is more of an explanation of how exceptional minds think and how brilliant decision-making occurs, not just in business but in real life.

# CHAPTER 3 SUMMARY

||||||||||||||||||||||||||

- Although it has long been accepted that there are cognitive skills that predict academic intelligence, it has mistakenly been assumed that no such skills exist that determine business intelligence.

- Academic intelligence measures (IQ tests) were created to assess a student's potential by testing skills in school subjects, such as arithmetic and vocabulary skills.

- Executive Intelligence focuses on the "subjects" of executive work, including: accomplishing tasks, working with and through other people, and assessing/adapting oneself.

- Just as one's proficiency in math is in large part determined by one's ability to add, subtract, multiply, and divide, there are specific cognitive skills that determine a person's success within each of the "subjects" of executive work.

- In order to be a "star," an individual must be highly capable in all three essential categories of executive work.

- Executive Intelligence determines the decision-making skill of those in leadership positions in any industry, in both the public and private sectors.

# CHAPTER 4

## Part One: The Competitive Advantage: Why Certain People Make the Difference

||||||||||||||||||||||||||

It has been well established that the quality of an organization's people is the essential determinant of its success. It is also clear that exceptional executive talent is scarce, and that identifying and cultivating the right people is paramount. But until now we have not had an understanding of the specific aptitudes that enable today's managers to excel in the global marketplace. Therefore, we have not been able to clearly identify and cultivate those leaders most capable of ensuring an organization's prosperity. It is this gap that the theory of Executive Intelligence seeks to close.

In his landmark work, *Good to Great,* Jim Collins studied corporations that had undergone a remarkable transformation, going from a history of mediocre performance to long-term profitability dramatically superior to that of their competitors. His "Great" leaders emphasized, above all, that the ultimate limitation on growth was the difficulty of attracting and keeping enough of the *right* talent.[1]

Jack Welch repeats a similar mantra when he describes how he built General Electric into the most-admired company in the world. His primary responsibility as CEO, he insists, was the identification and development of *star* executives throughout his business. He knew it would be

GE's stars that would determine the company's success or failure, and he devoted approximately 60 percent of his time to evaluating and cultivating GE's talent pool.[2]

Robert Johnson, chairman and CEO of BET, clarifies the key role these people play in a successful business:

"To me a star executive is a master of getting the right things done. They possess a disciplined mind and are very focused. They see what needs to get done and how best to get it done. Their presentations are logical and well reasoned, and they understand how to make your vision into a reality. So, as opposed to the people that just nod their heads and agree with you, when these executives throw up the caution flag, you pause and listen to their reasoning. Because most often they have good arguments regarding why something will hinder your ability to reach your goal. So you pay attention to them. Unfortunately, even though these people in large part determine your level of success, there's a real shortage of them, so they're hard to find."

As Johnson points out, finding and keeping exceptional people is a struggle that confronts every business. Dan Rosensweig, COO of Yahoo! Inc., details how his company has succeeded in maintaining its massive growth rate despite this challenge:

"No company is immune from the scarcity of great talent; that's why getting top people is Yahoo's number one concern. One of [Yahoo CEO] Terry Semel's great strengths is that from the beginning he knew it was the quality of the team around him that would determine Yahoo's success or failure. That in this highly dynamic, highly competitive environment, it is the strength of our *whole* team that determines our level of success.

> Nevertheless, we are realistic about how difficult it is to keep find-
> ing more great people. That's why we recognize that not every corpo-
> rate initiative is of equal priority. We constantly reevaluate so that the
> most important initiatives are being addressed by the right people. This
> is how Yahoo has been able to stay at the top of its game, despite its
> massive growth and the universal scarcity of quality human resources."

As Rosenweig explains, even the most successful companies are challenged to find sufficient numbers of skilled people. But Yahoo is careful
to make sure they maintain a highly talented workforce. So rather than
just fill their open positions with anyone who's available, they've adapted
their systems so that the most challenging and essential initiatives are always given to the people most qualified to handle them.

To be sure, the quality of an organization's people is an essential determinant of its success. But what is it about today's competitive environment that has made talent such an essential advantage? By clarifying how
the demands of executive work have changed, we can better understand
the abilities the best managers must possess. As we will see, the global nature of business today has altered traditional management models, making it crucial that superior Executive Intelligence exists throughout the
organization, not just at the top.

Peter Drucker, in his book *Managing In the Next Society,* describes
how one or two individuals used to be able to formulate a corporate strategy that would be viable for sometimes as long as twenty or thirty years.
General Motors, AT&T, and Sears, for example, had in the past succeeded
with long-term plans. But this, he warns, is no longer a viable option.[3]

Drucker points out that in the contemporary marketplace the accelerated pace of change requires constant adjustments to both overall strategy and execution. A CEO and his or her expert consultants can no
longer simply generate a linear blueprint for success and expect employ-

ees to effectively execute it step-by-step. Today far too many decisions and action plans must be formed and adjusted on the fly. It would be impossible for a single CEO to make so many adjustments in a timely way. As a result, corporations have been reorganized to spread authority and responsibility among many more people.

Andrea Jung, CEO of Avon, explains further:

"Decision-making in today's business environment is decentralized. Decisions are made at the local level, or at a functional or operating level. You can't grow a business around two to three good thinkers anymore, because your success depends on quality decisions from people at every level—salespeople, marketing people, strategy people, and so on. Everyone has to be able to think smart.

If you don't have the right amount of quality thinking in a complex growth company like ours, it is going to manifest itself in terms of marginalized discussions that rely upon wrong inputs and unskilled questions. And that's what drags down businesses. That's why companies that don't have good minds throughout their ranks get stuck at 100 million in revenue and don't get to 1 billion."

As Jung points out, this diffusion of decision-making responsibility has a downside. More decision makers are operating with no daily oversight, which means that managers with poor business judgment can have immediate and profound negative effects on a business. Mistakes often fester unnoticed, causing great harm. The expanded decision-making responsibilities of executives make it more important than ever that managers throughout organizations possess skilled judgment. The implication is that companies with more Executive Intelligence distributed throughout their senior ranks have a competitive advantage.

Kevin Rollins, the CEO of Dell Inc., for example, is clear about the benefit of having many talented executives working together:

> "We use such a collective way of thinking in order to improve upon each other's ideas that the end product is often very different from where we started. Take our printing and imaging business that is now doing very well: Michael Dell came up with the original idea, but we've had so much input and participation from leaders around the company that at this point it's a collective strategy rather than a strategy created by an individual. *That route and path to coming up with an ever-evolving and better strategy is the genius of the company.*
>
> What we've got right now is kind of like the Chicago Bulls of the 1990s. They had a critical mass of talent, and that allowed them to attain sustained periods of championship performance. That's why we're so tough about who we bring in. We've got to continually find new Michael Jordans and Scottie Pippens. We need a strong roster of players, because as a team we work better with the best talent pushing each other."

Peter Drucker notes an additional, equally important reason for why the "right" talent has become so crucial in today's environment: these are the people who determine how well your company uses the resources it has available. Drucker explains that wide access to equivalent physical and information resources means that those factors no longer provide much of a competitive advantage. In comparison to others, one company does not typically have superior access to raw materials, data, or physical plants. All these commodities can be readily purchased from any number of global suppliers. So, it is the more *productive* use of these resources that differentiates one organization's performance from another's.[4]

Jim Collins came to a similar conclusion. He found that "Great" performance companies did not have access to better data then their competitors, but that they consistently made more effective use of the same information. That is, they were able to understand the data and translate that understanding into actions that produced superior results. How well the resources are used, he concluded, depends on the decision-making capabilities of senior people throughout an organization. Once again, having the "right" people making these decisions has a profound impact on an organization's total performance. Collins describes these special people as uniquely capable of engaging in *disciplined* thought and *disciplined* action.[5]

Kevin Rollins describes how Dell's people built their extraordinarily successful business model by recognizing a new use for data that provided a decisive competitive advantage:

"We believe in substituting information for inventory. So anything we can do to streamline the flow of information up and down our supply chain means increased velocity and reduced inventory. Historically companies have shielded their information and not shared it with suppliers, because that might allow those suppliers to out-negotiate them. We have found that openly sharing information actually allows you to speed things up. The Internet accelerated this capability because you could get real-time information around the globe. And we realized that and said that's wonderful. Inventory is bad, information is good. So we used that information to speed the flow.

Now others are doing that as well. But that was one of the hallmarks of our supply-chain-management model. By combining customer knowledge with supplier knowledge, and applying that to our manufacturing process, we could wed the customer demands with

supplier availability in real time. This is how we replaced inventory
with information. And so our costs are lower."

Dell's notion of using data in order to eliminate inventory and reduce
costs is now legendary, and has been duplicated by many other businesses.
Its underlying logic is so sound that in hindsight it seems as though it
should have been obvious to others in the industry. But Dell was the first
to recognize how data could be used to dominate its competitors.

So how does one know if an individual manager is capable of contributing this type of sharp, effective thinking to a leadership team? The
works of Drucker, Welch, and Collins have provided important insights
into the instrumental role of executive decision-making in today's global
marketplace. But these business experts stopped short of delivering an
explicit description of the characteristics we seek.

Words like "right," "disciplined," or "star" clarify little. Those descriptions are like a police report stating there has just been a robbery at First
National Savings, so be on the lookout for a "bank robber." What you
need is a more specific identification: "Watch for a Caucasian female, in
her fifties, wearing a white coat, carrying two bags, and running down
Main Street."

So what is the "All Points Bulletin" that enables us to find the star executives? The theory of Executive Intelligence provides a specific description of those skills at the heart of exceptional business decision-making.
Once we identify the skills, we can determine the people who possess
them and place them in positions where their talent will do the most
good for the organization.

# Part Two: It Takes One to Know One

||||||||||||||||||||||||

The dramatic increase in the number of people with critical decision-making responsibilities is one reason that companies with more skilled executives outperform their competitors. But there is also another, more complex dynamic that gives these companies a decisive edge: they are able to create an atmosphere that demands, recognizes, and rewards these attributes. And why is this so crucial? Individuals with high Executive Intelligence cannot reach their peak performance unless surrounded by others with a similar level of skill.

Everyone's performance is enhanced or limited by the quality of the talent surrounding them. Professor Peter Senge of MIT's Sloan School of Management, in his much-cited 1990 work, *The Fifth Discipline: The Art and Practice of the Learning Organization*, repeatedly stressed the interdependent nature of individual performance within a corporation. Regardless of how strong one person's thinking is, without the help and support of others—to skillfully identify an idea's merit, to help improve it, and then to disseminate and implement it—that individual's best thinking will be lost. Senge's work suggests that a kind of organizational tipping-point exists, whereby an organization becomes capable of peak performance only when enough skilled people are brought together.[6]

Jack Welch also describes the importance of assembling a critical mass of talent at GE. To achieve the highest performance from your people, he counsels, you must create an environment where equally sharp individuals are brought together.

"We created an atmosphere where very bright people were encouraged and rewarded for sharing and challenging each other's ideas, and as a result we were able to reach new heights. To create an environment where the sum is greater than its parts, that's the challenge of management."

Dell Inc.'s leadership also recognizes how critical it is to have superior people throughout the organization in order to attain outstanding performance levels. Kevin Rollins explains:

"We have 'A' players throughout the organization, so we know good decisions and great ideas are going to flow out.

For instance, we used to maintain thirty days of inventory. We decided we needed to reduce that down to twenty-one days. But remarkably, the team in Europe figured out how to get it to fourteen days. We studied that and moved the rest of the world to fourteen days, then another one of our teams figured out how to move to seven. We just kept leapfrogging each other to levels of performance that we never imagined. This was possible because we have such talented people throughout our organization."

As Rollins makes clear, great performance is never the result of one individual operating in isolation. It arises from a collaborative effort.

In Mihaly Csikszentimihalyi's seminal book *Creativity*, he describes his study of the most brilliant works in history and his discovery that great thinking neither begins nor ends with a single individual. As Csikszentimihalyi researched the world's greatest innovations—including Charles Darwin's thesis on evolution, Thomas Edison's research with electricity, and Albert Einstein's formation of the Theory of Relativity—it became obvious to him that although these brilliant minds played an essential role, they were only one component of an entire system that helped inspire, evaluate, and propagate their momentous works.[7]

Csikszentimihalyi's point was further illustrated by his examination of one of the more fascinating anomalies in human history. Five celebrated works of artistic genius were created in Florence by five different artists between 1400 and 1425: Filippo Brunelleschi's dome of Florence Cathedral, Lorenzo Ghiberti's Gates of Paradise, Donatello's sculptures for the chapel of Orsanmichele, Masaccio's fresco cycle in the Brancacci Chapel, and the painting of the Adoration of the Magi by Gentile da Fabriano in the Church of the Trinity. While one might dismiss this artistic outpouring as a coincidence, Csikszentimihalyi's research revealed that these five masterpieces owed their existence to more than just chance.

In fact, he discovered that the Florentine churchmen, guild leaders, and bankers who commissioned these works were intensely involved in every stage of the creative process. Further, he found that these men were extremely skilled evaluators of artistic creations and gave meaningful feedback at all stages of the creative endeavor. The artists' final product reflected a highly iterative process in which, through collaboration, they were pushed beyond the limits of their initial ideas to create something that was not only unique but timeless in its beauty.[8]

It is interesting to note that the artists' initial proposals were not accepted. Their sponsors gave them highly specific feedback regarding ways in which the work needed to be elevated before it would be commissioned. While the individual talents of these artists were crucial, their work would never have achieved its historic stature without the active contributions of their unusually well informed patrons and audience.

Csikszentimihalyi's discoveries reinforce the notion that extraordinary performance is never an individual feat; it is inevitably a consequence of one person's collaboration with other exceptional thinkers. His conclusions highlight that together talented people can perform dramatically better than they ever could as individuals. Indeed, the whole is greater than the sum of its parts.

Both Collins and Welch point to similar processes in attaining peak performance in business. They cite *intense debate* as being crucial to finding the best answers. But such discussions would be fruitless—perhaps even counterproductive—if the participants were not adept at both separating good ideas from bad ones, and distinguishing meaningful directions from dead-end detours.

Dick Parsons, chairman and CEO of Time Warner, elaborates:

"You want to surround yourself with the best people you can, because being around smart people makes you better. When you have noncritical thinkers within the group, they are always chasing rabbits. They hinder the quality and the results of the discussion, because they ask the wrong questions or focus on the wrong issues. This can ultimately limit what you as a group can achieve."

As Parsons explains, the quality of the people involved in any collaboration can have a profound impact on the final product. So it is not enough to merely throw groups together and encourage them to challenge each other's thinking. Within these groups, the presence of unskilled thinkers, particularly in positions of authority, will often serve as serious impediments to getting optimal results—because inferior talent often fails to differentiate between the ideas that have merit and those that are misguided. Most of us have been involved in meetings where the group constantly drifts into discussing irrelevant considerations. Those members who are trying to maintain focus on key issues often become frustrated with these needless distractions and digressions.

In addition to diminishing the quality of discussions, unskilled leaders tend to be incapable of recognizing the stronger input of others. In 1999 Cornell University psychologists Justin Kruger and David Dunning performed a series of experiments examining highly skilled individuals and others who were grossly incompetent. They wrote about this research in an article titled "Unskilled and Unaware of It: How Difficulties Recognizing One's Own Incompetence Lead to Inflated Self-Assessments."[9]

In four separate studies Kruger and Dunning gave the subjects ability tests, including measures of their logical reasoning. They then had the participants assess their own performance on these tests, judge the answers of other individuals, and reassess their own ability after they had seen the responses of their peers.

They found that not only were the most incompetent individuals oblivious of their own poor performance, but they were also unable to recognize the superior decisions of others, even when the differences were dramatic. The worse their performance, the more exaggerated their self-perceptions became. For instance, those performing in the 12th percentile estimated themselves to be in the 62nd percentile of performance. The same deficiencies in their cognitive abilities that caused them to perform so poorly in the first place prevented them from recognizing the difference between their performance and that which is far superior to their own.

Lurita Doan, founder and CEO of New Technology Management, a leading security surveillance provider, explains:

> "It's so difficult to find the kind of people that will be the catalysts for the great things your company needs to achieve. The challenge is that everyone thinks they are one of these people—they really believe this.

If I were to have every person who walks through my door write down a list of their attributes, nearly every person would describe themselves as an innovative, outside-the-box thinker, a 'go-to' person with a 'can-do' attitude. They would all say, 'I'm creative, flexible, and innovative.' And they really believe it. But obviously this isn't reality. There are clearly differences in the talents and capabilities of individuals. And just because people tend to be blind to these differences does not make this any less true."

And weaker executives not only deliver poor results themselves but tend to negatively impact the quality of the work around them. The best reasoning can often be suppressed in an organization populated with unskilled thinkers. Csikszentimihalyi has stressed that too many obstacles placed in the way of good decision-making can easily breed frustration and apathy among the most capable people.[10] If executives are forced to function in an atmosphere that consistently fails to recognize and reward their most valuable suggestions, they will quickly become frustrated and lose the motivation to fight for what they believe to be right.

To achieve superior results, organizations must be populated with the most-capable thinkers. More often than not, however, skilled executives are surrounded by mediocre colleagues who overlook their best ideas. Over time this frustrates and alienates the most talented staff. And because talent is scarce, and organizations have not had appropriate means for evaluating and developing the stars in their midst, few companies have been able to achieve the critical mass required for peak performance.

# CHAPTER 4 SUMMARY

||||||||||||||||||||||||

- It has been well established that an organization's success depends upon the quality of its people, yet what makes a "quality" person has not been well understood.

- The global nature of business today has altered traditional management models, making it crucial that superior thinking skills exist throughout the organization, not just at the top.

- More decision makers are operating with no daily oversight, which means that managers with poor business judgment can have immediate and profound negative effects on a business.

- Companies with more Executive Intelligence distributed throughout their ranks have a competitive advantage, because they use available resources more effectively than their competitors.

- Less competent individuals are often blind to the superior thinking or ideas of others.

- Great thinking neither begins nor ends with a single person. Together talented people can perform dramatically better than they ever could as individuals.

# CHAPTER 5:

# Beyond Ideas:
# How Great Results
# Happen

*Execution,* or *follow-through,* is part of the business vernacular, and the concept has long been recognized as a key to leadership success. Every world-class CEO will speak at length about the need to not only conceptualize and formulate strategy but to see initiatives through to completion. Although the critical need for execution is universally accepted, the nuts and bolts of what makes some individuals dramatically more effective at this activity than others has been poorly understood.

A conversation about leadership with Jack Welch is punctuated with comments stressing the primary role of execution.

> "Big-shot leaders that I've seen fail are CEOs that express a strategy and think of it as gospel. But then they don't follow up. They don't challenge the results or see what happened after their first decree. They don't make adjustments based on what is actually happening. They just don't get into it. And rarely do things go in a straight line."

As Welch points out, the path from idea to execution is not linear. It is affected by so many unexpected factors that plans must always be adjusted on the fly. This is why templates, models, and managerial best-practices are woefully inadequate on their own. At the heart of one's ability to execute is the skill with which one can recognize and make these adjustments. In other words, the "smarts" that one can bring to bear on the unforeseen challenges of a particular plan determine the quality of the outcome.

Larry Bossidy, former chairman and CEO of Honeywell International, and management consultant Ram Charan joined together to write the national bestseller *Execution: The Discipline of Getting Things Done*. They challenged the notion that great leadership was primarily focused on high-level thinking, the communication of exciting visions, or the formation of strong personal bonds with people important to the business. Instead, they argued, *execution* is the central responsibility of any business leader, and effective execution requires a deep involvement with the substance and even the details of the business.[1]

Pat Russo, CEO of Lucent Technologies, discusses how important such involvement is:

> "Fifty-thousand-foot leaders [those that only focus on the big picture] get themselves into trouble. If you're not involved, you don't know what questions to ask of your people. I don't know what the CEO job is if it's not 'hands-on.' How can you run a company without an understanding of what's actually going on in the business?
>
> When I was running the Business Communications Systems Division at AT&T in the '90s, I was very focused on open communication. We had a very hierarchy-based culture, and I felt that people were nervous about speaking up. So I encouraged everyone, if they believed we were doing things that didn't make sense to the business, to first bring their concerns to their immediate boss. And I made it clear that if airing these concerns to their supervisor didn't get them anywhere,

they should call me directly. At the time this was considered heresy, because this was not the culture at AT&T.

I didn't get a lot of calls, but I did get a few, and they were very important. For instance, I once got a call from a woman who worked in one of our customer-service centers. We had just rearranged our regional sales structure and made some changes to the regional boundaries. She said, 'Pat'—and it sounded like she was scared to death—'I just have to tell you about something that we're doing that makes no sense to me. A year ago we moved a large group of customers into this service center and we've spent the last twelve months building strong relationships with them. We're doing really well and the customers are very satisfied. But I just heard that we are planning to move them out. I believe this is happening because of a turf issue with the regional sales heads.' I told her that I appreciated her raising this issue with me and that I'd look into it.

So I got the two regional sales heads on the phone and said, 'I understand that we are planning to move customers out of a service center that we moved them to just a year ago and into another. I don't know if this is true, but I'd really appreciate it if you could tell me what you have planned and why.' After some discussion, I concluded our conversation with 'I hear what you are saying, but I'm still not seeing how this benefits our customers.' Lo and behold, they came back to me with a new recommendation, concluding that it wasn't the best thing to do for the customers. That's a classic example of how the company could have done something very costly because two people were focused on their territories rather than on the best interests of our customers. If I was a fifty-thousand-leader, the woman from the Atlanta customer-service office never would have called, or I never would have listened. And we would have made a big mistake that would have upset our customers."

Pat Russo's story shows how great leaders remain deeply involved in their businesses by asking the tough questions and challenging their people's thinking. This practice is also cited as essential by Bossidy and Charan, who describe great leadership as a systematic process of rigorously discussing what is happening, what should be happening, and how things are getting done, along with follow-up questions that ensure accountability from those involved. "Only a leader can ask the tough questions that everyone needs to answer," they write, "then manage the process of debating the information and making the right trade-offs. And only the leader who's intimately engaged in the business can know enough to have the comprehensive view and ask the tough incisive questions."[2]

This does not mean that executives must know how to perform every job in their company. But they must know enough of the details to be able to challenge and ensure the soundness of their people's decisions. Jack Welch, referring to his time at GE, explains:

"There's no way I'd know how to design a piece of medical equipment. But I'd know the competitive environment, where this equipment might fit, and whether or not the resources my people were asking for made sense. That was my responsibility, even though I obviously wasn't the one designing the machine."

Welch, Bossidy, and Charan all suggest that it is a leader's capacity for sharp and challenging dialogue that determines how well he or she executes a strategy. "Such dialogue," Bossidy and Charan point out, "is the basic unit of work . . . and it is through such constructive back and forth that work actually gets done."[3] Without this kind of dialogue, leaders fail. And the quality of the dialogue, they conclude, depends on the abilities of the leader.

Jack Welch elaborates:

"If you've got someone who is naïve and doesn't have these skills and somehow got the top job, they can't follow up well and ask good questions. Therefore, they don't know when they are being 'had.' It's about seeing the holes *and* getting through them, seeing the opportunity *and* capitalizing on it. This requires an intense discussion and healthy skepticism about what your people are going to do."

As Welch points out, meaningful dialogue involving intense discussion and healthy skepticism is essential for success. But how are leaders like Jack Welch consistently able to make these discussions so useful? In other words, what are the skills that allow them to do this so exceptionally well? Amazingly, when posed with this question, star executives generally refer to broad concepts such as instinct or business acumen. To a large extent the best leaders remain unaware of the specific aptitudes that make them so much better at execution than their colleagues. Yet differences obviously exist.

When it comes to execution, the skill with which activities are accomplished is what differentiates star talent. For instance, in the case of professional basketball players, we all know the things they must do—scoring, helping teammates score, and defending against their opponents. But why do some of them perform so much better than their peers? In basketball it comes down to specific aptitudes, such as foot speed, jumping ability, and reaction time. These are the raw abilities that differentiate professional athletes.

In business, there are certain raw abilities that are central to success as well. It is the quality of the questions executives ask, the skill with which they evaluate the information they are given, and how well they anticipate the likely consequences of actions that distinguish star talent. These abilities are all components of Executive Intelligence, and the best executives rely upon these skills and build organizations that value them. That is how they consistently out-execute their peers.

Norm Wesley, chairman and CEO of Fortune Brands, created a company that did just that. Fortune Brands is a leading consumer-products company and is the parent company of many of the top names in various product categories, including Jim Beam bourbon, Titleist golf balls and clubs, and Moen faucets. During Wesley's tenure, the company has consistently outperformed other leading consumer companies and the broader market.

Since he became CEO at the end of 1999, Fortune Brands' sales have increased from $5.5 billion to more than $7 billion in 2004. Over that time, total shareholder returns—including stock price and dividends— have increased at an annualized rate of 21 percent, in contrast to minus 4 percent for the S&P 500. That includes a stock price that has grown from $33 to more than $80. Wesley says sharp, constructive dialogue has played a central role in the exceptional results of Fortune Brands.

> "While our first priority is internal growth, we've also made several high-return acquisitions. But even though intellectually an acquisition can sound great, it comes down to whether you can actually execute and deliver on these plans. A big part of our excellent track record is we have such a tough, open dialogue. Before we make any purchase we've tested whether we can actually operationally make it happen. The truth has been seriously tested. This is a big driver of our success."

Wesley also comments on the role a leader plays in guiding this dialogue and how he delves beneath the surface to uncover the critical truths:

"I learned how to do this from one of my first bosses and mentors. He had a huge influence on my professional development as a leader. His style was what I'd call a 'prober.' He'd insist on methodically asking questions, pushing and probing people's assumptions. Before I understood what he was really doing, I'd get impatient and want to move on to the next topic. But I soon learned how crucial his challenges were. He'd consistently reveal that the reality of a situation under discussion was very different from how it was being presented.

Another critical influence on my development was a boss and mentor that I'd call a 'grenade launcher.' He'd say things that would intentionally cause controversy and force people into tough discussions.

Now, neither of these is my own particular style. I'm a numbers guy. I recognize the discrepancies when numbers and dialogue don't match. But while we all have different styles, we each have the same purpose—to get to the truth and find out what is really going on. You have to get beneath the surface.

For instance, we were looking at a potential overseas acquisition that seemed like a real fit for one of our divisions. On the surface it appeared terrific. It had a great brand and was positioned well in a high-end market. And it would give us a huge presence in a country where we were really looking to expand. So my division head and I flew over there to talk to them. Through our conversations it quickly became clear that their management team was not at all realistic about the challenges confronting their business and its cost structures. They simply were not asking each other the tough questions regarding the realities confronting their business. But even worse, they seemed totally unwilling to engage in the tough questioning that would expose these issues. We could not acquire this company and have any faith that their leadership could recognize and execute what needed to be done in order to be successful. So we withdrew from the bidding."

Wesley believes so strongly in the importance of such back-and-forth discussions that in 1999 he moved Fortune Brands' corporate headquarters from Connecticut to Chicago in order to be closer to its affiliated companies. Being closer geographically eased many of the logistical barriers to maintaining these conversations, which he considers a central part of their corporate culture. His decision to transfer the offices reflects the priority he places on close cooperation and dialogue in order to ensure world-class execution across all of Fortune Brands. Wesley's decision is a tangible example of the observations made by Welch, Bossidy, and Charan of the necessity to create an environment that fosters participatory, challenging dialogue as a means of reaching new heights and achieving objectives.

The insights of these management experts help to illuminate how the best leaders successfully follow through in their businesses. By focusing on the fundamental skills behind such achievements, we can more accurately compare executive talent. Without such an understanding, we will never be able to ensure that decision-making responsibility is given to those best able to deliver. The theory of Executive Intelligence finally defines those skills central to effective execution.

# CHAPTER 5 SUMMARY

||||||||||||||||||||||||||

- Execution, or follow-through, has been identified as an essential responsibility of any business leader.

- Executive Intelligence not only allows one to develop a successful strategy; it also directly influences the effectiveness with which an executive sees a project through to completion.

- Every plan requires adjustment and modification to overcome the unforeseen challenges that inevitably arise. For the effective execution of a strategy, an executive must have a deep involvement with the substance and even the details of the business.

- Great leaders remain deeply involved in their businesses by asking the tough questions and challenging their people's thinking through a systematic process of rigorously discussing what is happening, what should be happening, and how things are being done.

- It is a leader's capacity for this pointed dialogue that determines how well he or she executes a strategy.

# WHY IS EXECUTIVE INTELLIGENCE SO RARE?

# CHAPTER 6

## Part One:
## The Executive
## Intelligence Gap

||||||||||||||||||||||||||

When it comes to hiring executives, the multitude of existing leadership theories have confused and distracted us from focusing on key selection criteria. As a result, we now have many very bad executives mixed with some good ones. To understand the magnitude of the problem, we need to gauge how good the current managerial population is at the critical skills that comprise Executive Intelligence. Unfortunately, the answer to that question, according to recent research on this topic, is disheartening.

In 2002, Warren Buffett remarked on the dearth of skilled executives when he explained why he decided Jim Kilts should be the next CEO of Gillette after only one meeting. "If you listen to Jim analyze a business situation . . . everything he says makes sense—and frankly, finding someone like that is a *rarity*."[1] Buffett is far from alone in his assessment of the disturbing lack of business judgment among executives.

Dick Parsons of Time Warner, comments about the scarcity of such leaders:

"The truly insightful people that can really get to the right place are quite rare. There exists a continuum, but the talented ones are very tough to find. Many executives have trouble dealing with complexity. They get lost in data and are unable to pull back and see what's really important."

As Parsons points out, executives capable of the most useful insights are few and far between.

In a 1995 study performed by human resource specialists Yankelovich/ Kepner-Tregoe, three hundred senior executives were asked about their peers' decision-making skills.[2] Eighty percent of the executives felt that their peers frequently failed to achieve their objectives. Half the executives surveyed had no confidence that their colleagues could ask the appropriate questions necessary to guide their actions. And 49 percent of the executives rated their peers as a 3 or less on a 6-point scale when it came to understanding critical issues in complex situations. Clearly, lack of Executive Intelligence is seen as a problem, by both leading management experts and the majority of working executives.

Ironically, although a high percentage of executives perceive their colleagues' Executive Intelligence as weak, they are unlikely to acknowledge their own deficiencies. Individuals with weak cognitive skills are rarely aware of their limitations. In fact, they tend to dramatically inflate their own performance, as the Cornell University studies of Justin Kruger and David Dunning,[3] discussed in chapter 4 of this book, illustrate.

Further, prominent leadership experts have consistently cited poor executive judgment as the most important factor in corporate failure. Dartmouth's Sydney Finkelstein conducted an in-depth study of some of the most devastating corporate mistakes in modern history. In each of his case studies, alarmingly poor decision-making played an essential role in the disastrous results.[4]

The deficiencies shared by these failed leaders included their inability to recognize competitive pressures, their failure to appreciate the vital importance of certain information, and their weakness in acknowledging and correcting mistakes (both their own and the mistakes of others). Unfortunately, all too often individuals are given tremendous authority over large amounts of human and capital resources even when they lack the cognitive skills needed to run a company well.

Ian Mitroff, winner of the Harold Quinton Distinguished Chair in Business Policy at the University of Southern California, maintains that all serious errors of management can be traced to one fundamental flaw—muddled thinking. In his book *Smart Thinking for Crazy Times,* Mitroff cited many examples of executives who failed to recognize the assumptions guiding their decisions, who ignored alternative perspectives, or who disregarded the probable unintended consequences of their actions.[5] His case studies made a consistent and persuasive argument that without these skills, leaders are ill-equipped to confront the complexities of the business environment. Typically, they are overmatched by competitors who have better-thought-out plans of action and the skills needed to execute them.

Bob Davies, the CEO of Church & Dwight, an international manufacturer of commercial-, home-, and personal-care products that has outperformed the S&P and Dow by nearly triple under Davies's ten-year tenure, discusses this challenge:

> "You are not just looking for bright or accomplished people. You need people with highly skilled judgment who are effective at making things happen. But finding these people is extraordinarily hard to do."

Stephen Carter, former CEO of Cingular Wireless and current CEO of data-cabling-products manufacturer Superior Essex, where he has engineered an impressive turnaround, comments on how hard it is to find skilled executives:

"As a leader, what we're always looking for are the people who will bring you the jewel and not the lump of coal. But it's rare to come across these people. Unfortunately, there are a lot of people that spend an awful lot of time saying a whole lot of nothing."

Today we have a population of executives who, on the whole, do not possess the essential skills necessary to render thoughtful, disciplined action. Nor are they likely to realize how inferior their thinking is. As a result, we have too many business leaders who are prone to taking action without thinking. Further, most executives are completely unaware of the costs of their "shoot first" attitude. There is a pervasive, misguided belief that thoughtful analysis is an obstacle to quick results.

# Part Two: No Time to Think—
# The Myth About Speed

||||||||||||||||||||||||||

Picture Auguste Rodin's sculpture *The Thinker,* which was unveiled in 1906 in front of Rome's Pantheon. It depicts a muscular young man sitting with his chin resting on his hand, pondering endlessly. Unfortunately, this is how most in the business community have come to view critical thought. Critical thinkers are assumed to be frozen statues incapable of action or, in the popular vernacular, suffering from "paralysis by analysis." This misunderstanding has led to a polarized notion that swift action cannot coexist with reasoned thought.

"Speed, speed, speed" is the mantra of countless CEOs, which has led to the generalization that speed in itself is a virtue. But that is not true. Making a quick decision when the situation calls for it is essential. In other circumstances, however, taking more time to collect data and ask the right questions is even more necessary. Yet such distinctions have been lost, as *fast* has become synonymous with *good,* and *slow* with *bad.*

If you stop to really consider this popular myth, you realize that both *fast* and *slow* are neutral descriptions until they are considered within the context of a specific situation. Blanket rules, such as "act, act, act," are appealing in their simplicity. But simple does not mean appropriate. Careful analysis of a situation may call for urgency and a fast verdict—or it may identify a need for a slower, more deliberate process. But regardless of the speed with which action is taken, weighing the factors in order to reach that decision requires skilled thinking.

Irene Rosenfeld, CEO of Frito-Lay, tells of an experience that illustrates this notion:

"I call it 'go slow to go fast.' Because we know speed is of the essence, too often we immediately start moving without first taking the time to think about what we're trying to accomplish.

There are hundreds of stories about this. Everyone is trying to act quickly, but too often they run out to solve a problem without fully understanding what problem they are trying to solve. This creates a lot of organizational angst which slows things down and leads to all sorts of issues regarding job satisfaction and work-life balance.

For instance, we have a promotion going with one of our customers right now. We chose not to flag the offer on the front of the Doritos bag so that it wouldn't upset our other customers. So we only put the offer on the back of the bag. And now we're hearing that the offer is not as impactful as it could be.

So my team had a discussion about how *quickly* we could redo the packaging to make the offer more prominent. But the packaging solution being proposed would have contorted our organization for weeks. It suddenly dawned upon me that maybe we weren't focusing on the right thing. I asked them, 'Isn't it just a question of how to tell people to go to the back of the Doritos bag? Because once they get to the bag and turn it over, we're just fine. The issue is that they just don't know to go to the back of the bag.'

That led us to talk about in-store radio, in-store signage, newspaper ads—all simple things that we could quickly and easily do, as opposed to changing the packaging, which would require getting new roll stock, and writing-off all the old packaging."

As Rosenfeld's story highlights, brilliant answers can be generated instantaneously or take much more deliberation. And horribly misguided thinking can be delivered even after extensive contemplation. But regardless of the circumstances, speed in itself is not the prerequisite for good decisions. It is choosing the appropriate speed for a given circumstance that is one of the most essential components of executive decision-making.

When CEOs call for speed, what they are talking about is attaining the **right** objective as quickly as possible. A highly committed workforce can contribute countless hours of overtime running full speed toward a given target. But if that goal is ill-conceived, the result will be a costly, or even fatal, delay.

As Rick Lenny, chairman, president, and CEO of the Hershey Company, points out, speed is always a factor, but how quickly you act should depend on the circumstances.

"It's a notion of guardrails—recognizing how fast or slow one needs to go depends on the situation. We may all *want* perfect information before we act, but there's just no such thing. Knowing how much information is enough in order to act is the key. At Hershey, we talk about at what point we've learned enough to go do something. Often, the longer one waits before doing something the more detrimental it is to the chances of success. For instance, when structuring customer promotions, we permit wider guardrails, therefore we can move at a faster pace. But when contemplating an acquisition, the guardrails narrow, and more information is required. This necessitates moving more carefully. It's the leader's job to know when to step on the accelerator or the brake."

Lenny describes the important considerations any great leader must take into account with regard to speed and action. But what is it that allows some managers to accomplish this so much more effectively than their peers? What is the mechanism that allows them to do this? It's not as if Rick Lenny and other extraordinary CEOs are applying a checklist to their decisions. The deftness with which they apply their cognitive skills is instinctive and natural. In other words, it's a form of intelligence. There's simply no way to codify their decision-making process into a step-by-step guide.

Checklists, such as those found in management textbooks, are almost never actually applied on the job. That is because the nature of executive decision-making involves infinite immediate judgments that render these handbooks impractical. Inevitably, executives are forced to rely upon their on-the-spot analysis to know when to press for more information and when to demand action.

Dick Parsons, CEO of Time Warner, explains further:

> "Textbooks teach people subject matter, but they don't teach them how to think. And I would say that the ability to look at complex problems and break them into manageable parts is much more important. People need to be able to do that instantly, in the moment. That capability is just not one you can get from a book. But these are the skills you really need."

Clearly one's ability to analyze and process information is not something that can be accomplished with a checklist. Similarly, an outline of Executive Intelligence skills is merely a description of the abilities that allow stars to meet their objectives. They are aptitudes that one possesses, not a guidebook that one can follow. There is no application sequence or time component attached to them; they happen instantly and simultaneously. For example, when responding to a particular directive, someone with high Executive Intelligence is instantly *processing the underlying as-*

*sumptions* involved or instinctively *noting if there are any flaws in the suggestions being made*. This all happens automatically, as star executives go directly to the essentials of the matter at hand, as well as related considerations. That is the nature of Executive Intelligence: it concerns the quality of one's judgment process.

When Michael Jordan took a shot in basketball, he never ran through a checklist of skills before he actually released the ball. His innate abilities constantly adapted to take advantage of the flow of the game. His perception of the other players and his feel for the ball and orientation to the basket all took place instantaneously. It would be impossible to schematically diagram the underlying aptitudes that enabled Michael Jordan to be the best in his profession. But by dissecting and understanding the individual skills that combined to allow Jordan to execute well—his physical speed, his leaping ability, his eye-hand coordination—we can begin to understand how to evaluate and improve our own game.

Like a star basketball player, a star executive does not consciously select from a list of skills he or she needs to apply. Instead certain skills come to the forefront as a natural response to the situation at hand. These instantaneous reactions are at the core of executive performance. Regardless of the strategy that has been created, as Jack Welch pointed out earlier, business is never purely linear. Executives must always make necessary strategic corrections or detours. And these decisions happen moment to moment. As Rick Lenny of Hershey explains:

> "We teach a course in strategic thinking where we caution that fact-finding and situation appraisal are only part of the equation; it's the 'science' part. What I'm talking about is the 'art' part—how one takes information and converts it *in the moment* into insights and into action. That's what really determines one's success."

Yes, it is crucial to move as quickly as a situation will allow, but driving full speed in the wrong direction can send an organization straight off a cliff. And the aptitude with which an executive recognizes the speed required to make a decision is largely influenced by his or her level of Executive Intelligence. For instance, *differentiating essential objectives from less relevant concerns, critically examining the accuracy of assumptions about what needs to be done, and appropriately considering the probable effects of an action* all play a role in determining the right decision at the right time.

Skilled executives do not always take their time, nor do they always act instantly. They use their cognitive skills to determine what is appropriate for the situation.

Jim Kilts, the CEO of Gillette, explains:

> "Whatever the situation, you have to operate from a sound basis—you have to think. Otherwise, when you execute your plan, you may be bouncing your way off of one wall and into another."

It all seems so simple. You use your cognitive skills to determine where you go and how fast you need to get there. It seems that everyone should be able to do this, but that is not the case. The vast majority of executives almost never pause to think before they act. This bias toward taking immediate action with little regard for the consequences dominates executive behavior. In short, we have a workforce of managers who use little if any critical thought as they go about their jobs.

# Part Three:
# Action Without Thought—
# The Reality of
# Executive Behavior

||||||||||||||||||||||||||

One of the most-published authors on managerial decision-making, McGill University professor Henry Mintzberg, wrote a book titled *The Nature of Managerial Work* that was published in 1973 and remains one of the most-influential discussions on the subject of business thinking. He brought together the findings of hundreds of studies involving senior and middle managers, hospital administrators, and structured observations of the work of chief executives. His in-depth analysis revealed that managers rarely employ rational or linear approaches to problem solving and almost never make decisions by first trying to understand what the actual problem is that they are addressing. Instead, he found that they typically take immediate action, groping their way toward a solution through trial and error. Mintzberg's research revealed that acting without thinking is how the vast majority of managers do their jobs.[6]

Andrea Jung, CEO of Avon, explains why executives so often act without thinking:

"The pace of business is furious. The textbook leadership process and the real process are not the same. Problems come quickly, not in slow motion. That is the source of why there is so much 'ready, fire, then aim.' But you have to maintain decision-making rigor, because when you lose that, and you're just winging it, that's when problems generally happen. The loss of this discipline is what is responsible for so many people jumping without thinking."

Harvard Business School's Daniel Isenberg reached a similar conclusion in his 1984 *Harvard Business Review* article on how senior managers solve problems.[7] For two years Isenberg studied the thought processes of more than a dozen senior executives while they were on the job. He observed them, conducted extensive interviews with their coworkers and subordinates, and questioned them about their thinking as they went about doing their work. He discovered that rather than use systematic approaches that involved even brief analysis, the senior managers he studied would act first and then examine the results of their efforts. Overwhelmingly, they used trial and error to choose an approach and come up with a solution.

In 1986 during a follow-up study, Isenberg employed a variety of methods to more fully understand how twelve general managers solved problems.[8] For instance, he gave them case-study situations and asked them to identify the problem and what they would do about it. Again, he witnessed a propensity to act without undertaking any critical inquiry. Often the study participants would begin suggesting solutions before they'd been given half the information, even though they were under no time pressure and more information was clearly forthcoming. Their analyses were cursory and based on personal experience with similar problems. They often chose a course of action simply so they could learn more about an issue, and then used the results to look for other solutions. Again, Isenberg's work highlights that when making decisions, executives jump to immediate conclusions, and then depend overwhelmingly on trial-and-error learning. Critical thought plays little role, if any, in their activities.

Gillette's CEO, Jim Kilts, laughed when I asked if he could think of an example that highlights the tendency of executives to act without thinking.

> "Probably one every day . . . One I can think of right away involved the reorganization of the sales force at Nabisco. A consulting firm had come in and done a big study. They told Nabisco they could save $60 million if they could eliminate the dual role of the sales rep, and divide the existing sales force into two separate jobs. One would be purely responsible for selling, and the other would be responsible for servicing the customer.
>
> So that's what Nabisco did. They figured, 'Well, we need to save some money and using this model would save $60 million, so let's do it.'
>
> But those responsible for the decision never questioned the assumption that separating sales and service roles was a good idea. It turned out that once they separated the two roles, people did *neither* well. Those who were selling couldn't get customers to listen to them because the service part was so screwed up. But the salespeople couldn't explain why the service part was screwed up because they no longer had responsibility for it. It was no longer their problem.
>
> The customers only wanted to see one face; they wanted one person in charge of their store. So when Nabisco divided executional responsibility, they never critically examined the assumptions under the new model. It was contrary to what the customer wanted, and it was contrary to what Nabisco could practically manage. That one was really costly."

Jim Kilts laments the fact that it is so common for business executives to act without thinking. In his view, the problem derives from the widely accepted fallacy that as long as managers are busy, they are doing their jobs well, even though they may often be committing their time and resources to actions that are unlikely to be fruitful, and may even be counterproductive.

No matter the costs of such action-first behavior, in most cases it is encouraged and even rewarded. When Karen Jehn and Keith Weigelt of the Wharton School studied decision-making styles, they demonstrated that managers, particularly in Western cultures, have a high regard for anyone who orders immediate action.[9] The very act of taking charge in pursuit of a goal is appealing. Unfortunately, few skills are applied to ensure that these actions are the best way to reach the right goal.

In this environment, individuals who pause to question actions or goals risk being considered "hesitant to take charge." Workplace norms that scream "Don't think—Act!" have supported these behaviors.[10] Denigrating thoughtful action helps perpetuate a system that neither recognizes the necessity of critical thinking skills nor nurtures their development.

Bob Davies, CEO of Church & Dwight, explains why:

> "We make heroes of CEOs who are decisive, bold, and brazen. We write stories about them. But an effective CEO must want the company to be successful far more than he or she wants to personally be seen as 'right,' heroic, or popular."

While this brazenness is often mistaken for strong leadership, the consequences can be deadly and not just to business success. Take for example one of the most heroic rescues in the history of the American military, as recounted by author Hampton Sides in his critically acclaimed work *Ghost Soldiers*.[11] Hampton describes how a small American force was able to liberate American prisoners that were about to be slaughtered by their Japanese captors on the islands of the Philippines.

In January 1945, near the end of World War II, the tide had turned aggressively against the Japanese army. The Americans were sweeping across the Pacific, and were preparing to take back control of the Philippines.

At the Cabanatuan POW camp, the 513 American prisoners interned there were facing intensifying danger. Japanese commanders were under standing orders to slaughter any POWs in their control if the battle situation ever became "urgent." The advancing American troops had learned of this policy from the eleven American survivors of another major POW camp in the Philippines, the camp at Palawan, where in December of 1944, 139 American prisoners were shot, bayoneted, or burned alive by their Japanese captors.

A rescue mission was launched ahead of the advancing American army in a desperate attempt to save the Americans at Cabanatuan from the same fate. With the help of local Filipino rebels, 121 U.S. Rangers launched a surprise attack on the camp, freeing the men interned there. But while this initial assault was risky, the task of escorting the rescued prisoners to safety was even more daunting. Most of them were injured, sick, and weak, and had to endure a march of over thirty miles, with local Japanese forces giving chase.

Of greatest concern was a battalion of one thousand Japanese troops that was stationed less than a mile northeast of the prison camp. Preventing them from joining in the battle, and thereby cutting off the American's escape, was crucial to the mission's success. But this was a seemingly impossible task. The Japanese troops far outnumbered the American and Filipino forces and were in possession of tanks and other heavy equipment. But there was no choice—at all costs these Japanese troops had to be prevented from pursuing the escaping prisoners.

Responsibility for this task fell to U.S. Ranger colonel Henry A. Mucci and Filipino rebel commander Juan Pajota. They approached the Japanese camp from the south. The camp was located on the north bank of a river with only a single bridge, the Cabu bridge, as the crossing point. The Japanese position was remarkably vulnerable to attack. The rangers and rebels surprised the Japanese, firing into the camp from the south bank. The Japanese commander, Tomeo Oyabu, immediately ordered his men across the bridge to confront their attackers, whom they outnumbered ten to one. But Pajota had positioned his forces in a giant V, focusing all their fire on the bridge. Every charging Japanese soldier was cut down to a man. Yet, Oyabu never paused. He sent a second wave of men, and then a third. All were annihilated.

During the firefight, Colonel Mucci began to prepare to reposition his men to meet a change in the Japanese commander's tactics. Surely, he thought, Oyabu would realize the folly of his rush to direct confrontation and look for alternative routes to attempt a flanking maneuver. He relayed his thoughts to Captain Pajota, who calmly shook his head. Pajota knew Oyabu too well. "They will keep coming," Pajota replied, "He [Oyabu] knows no other way."[12] The totally ineffective, suicidal response of the Japanese commander continued, resulting in a horrible carnage, with hundreds and hundreds of bodies piling up, until the entire Japanese unit was virtually annihilated.

Oyabu was determined to confront his attacking foes with a fearless charge. His failure to think, in a situation where he had clearly been outmaneuvered, was his downfall. He did what so many leaders do when confronting a problem: he charged full speed ahead without pausing to consider the best way to reach his objectives.

Jim Collins underscored the rarity of thoughtful action in corporate America when he found that one of the key differences separating great companies from those that remained mired in mediocrity was their culture of "Discipline." He stressed that discipline meant more than just demanding that people take action; it had to do with getting people to first engage in disciplined thought and then take disciplined action. Collins cited Walgreen's approach to the Internet boom as an example.[13]

Walgreen's executives refused to follow their competitors in a mad rush to get "wired." Instead they insisted on a deliberate, methodical approach: they paused, critically reflected, and identified a highly effective plan for using the Internet to improve their competitive position. To quote Collins's playfully sarcastic remark: "They decided to use their brains. They decided to think!"[14]

But as Collins points out, Walgreen's deliberative process represented a departure from the normal behavior of most companies, whose executives are expected to act now and ask questions later. If speed were the sole objective, this approach would have more merit. But getting to the *right* answer as fast as possible is the key to success. Reviewing relevant information—using probing questions and on-the-spot, careful deliberation—lacks the immediate "launch into action" mode that we delude ourselves is necessary in today's fast-paced world. These activities, however, are ultimately the quickest approach to achieving optimal results.

Dell Inc.'s leaders have proven themselves able to make thoughtful, deliberate moves that yield positive results far faster than their competitors. While Dell's leaders are acutely aware of the crucial need for speed in today's competitive environment, their understanding of how to actually deliver such speed is unique. Kevin Rollins, Dell's CEO, describes how Dell goes about balancing speed with sound reasoning:

"We believe a strategy does not have to be completely baked before launch. However, we do not believe in hunches. So with a foundation of analytics and good data and good assessment, we will launch. And we will fine-tune and correct along the way. Though we want to get moving fast, the difference between our method and the 'gut' launch is that there is a lot of data analyzed. We don't want to protract the data assessment/analytic phase, we want to get moving. So we do a lot of experiments, learn, refine, and then go. But we only do this if we feel the idea has potential after our initial analysis.

For instance, we made the decision to enter printing and imaging, networking and consumer electronics—because the data showed that our model would work. We said this looks pretty good, and it has all the characteristics of a good one. So let's launch it, and we'll refine it as we go. But we don't do things on hunches or gut instincts at Dell. Everything we try comes from a sound analytic base."

Rollins is referring to Dell's use of critical thinking at every stage of their strategy-development-and-execution cycle. Their extraordinary pace of implementation proves that critical analysis does not hinder quick decision-making. Yet with today's emphasis on speed, sound analysis has been overlooked and unreasonably maligned despite the crucial role it plays in success. Critical inquiry is all too often seen as an impediment, when in reality it must be acknowledged as a catalyst of effective action. Any sound analysis should always include recognition of the time constraints involved, the depth of analysis required to make a good decision, and the potential cost of lost opportunity. Those factors create a natural guide to how complete the analysis should be, and they allow the circumstances to determine the scope of one's deliberations.

The delusion that critical thought is a hindrance to fast results has never been more dangerous to corporate success. Action-oriented managers often argue they do not have time to get something right the first time, yet somehow they find the time to redo it three or four times.[15] In an accelerated business environment, you have one shot, not three, to get a decision right. And just as a good golf swing takes no more time than a bad one, the good swing gets you to the hole much more quickly. Asking the right questions when facing a complex decision is no more time-consuming than asking the wrong ones. In fact, it saves time. Yet few executives can perform such critical inquiries. Why are these skills so rare?

# CHAPTER 6 SUMMARY

||||||||||||||||||||||||||

- The multitude of existing leadership theories has confused and distracted us from focusing on key performance criteria. As a result, we have a managerial population that as a whole is weak in Executive Intelligence.

- Surveys have shown that 80 percent of executives feel that their peers frequently fail to achieve their objectives, and half of those surveyed had no confidence that their colleagues could ask the appropriate questions needed to take proper action.

- Prominent leadership experts have consistently cited poor executive judgment as the most important factor in corporate failures.

- Too many business leaders take action without thinking and are completely unaware of the costs of this tendency.

- Critical thinking has become synonymous with "paralysis by analysis," while taking immediate action has been mistakenly characterized as a uniformly positive practice.

- Speed itself is not a prerequisite for good decisions; it is choosing the *appropriate* speed for a given situation that is one of the most essential components of executive decision-making.

- Executives often take immediate action, groping their way toward a solution through trial and error, and such action-first behavior is generally encouraged and even rewarded.

- Asking the right questions when facing a complex decision is no more time-consuming than asking the wrong ones.

# CHAPTER 7

# Part One:
# Blame It on the Brain

The action-first orientation of most executives is not due to their laziness or incompetence. In fact, the vast majority of these individuals are giving their earnest best efforts. In order to fully understand why their good intentions often fall so short, we must look for the root cause of this pervasive problem. Examination of normal human cognition reveals that people, without rigorous training, do not naturally develop a high level of Executive Intelligence. In fact, the way our minds process information leads humans to draw unwarranted conclusions again and again.

The near universal preference for trial-and-error decision-making is a result of the unique architecture of the brain. Action is instinctive—a consequence of brain functions that have evolved over millions of years. Consider the environment in which human intellect developed. The primitive mind was contending with constant, serious threats to survival. The propensity for immediate action was an advantage when it came to escaping danger at the sound of a snapping twig or the sight of an animal unexpectedly lunging.

Though we no longer face the same perils, many of the brain's instinctual patterns persist as we work to make sense of our chaotic world. For instance, when crossing the street, we jump at the sound of screeching brakes; our minds are reflexively protecting us from some perceived danger. Similarly, when we make a suggestion to our executive committee and a colleague criticizes our idea, our instincts scream, "defend yourself." They do not urge us to understand the substance of the criticism. That kind of instinctual brain function, however, serves as an impediment to skilled executive behavior.

The structure behind our intelligence is not arbitrary but dictated at least in part by our need to draw instant conclusions about the world around us.[1] However, a brain that quickly draws conclusions about what is going on and causes the body to immediately react was much more useful to our ancestors than it is to us in a complex, modern environment. Today, when it comes to competing in the business world, our mind's predilection for drawing instant conclusions and leaping into immediate action is often more of a hindrance than a help. Skillful handling of these complex situations requires, instead, a high degree of careful logic, and this aptitude was not accentuated during the brain's evolution.

Scholar Jeremy Campbell, author of several books about human cognition, wrote an extraordinary work titled *The Improbable Machine*, describing how the first computer scientists set out to construct processors that could imitate human intelligence. They built computers to solve problems using deductive reasoning and then added millions of lines of code to teach them rules of logic that would guide that reasoning. But these computers were incapable of performing anything but the very narrow task for which they were programmed. And although scientists were eventually able to build supercomputers that could outplay humans in a constrained, rule-based game such as chess, the same machines were easily confounded by other basic tasks. The machines turned out to be so astonishingly narrow in their expertise that they could hardly be called intelligent.[2]

No matter how many rule-based codes the engineers tried to program, these computers could not make the simplest generalizations across topics without severe errors. The fundamental cause of this dead end? The scientists were assuming that logic was the core driver of human intelligence. But it turns out that the human mind has no inherent system of logic. In fact, the human brain is consistently, systematically *illogical.*[3]

And this is for good reason, since logic would be a hopeless foundation for human intelligence. Logic follows a careful, wholly consistent sequence of rules; a contradiction in any part of the sequence causes the whole system to crumble. Logic cannot tolerate inconsistency or significant gaps in knowledge.[4] Yet our world is full of seeming inconsistencies, contradictions, and unknowns. For instance, seemingly a ship constructed of steel, or even carved out of rock, should not be able to float. An aircraft weighing two hundred tons should not be able to fly; an ant should not be able to lift five times its body weight. Clear water should not look blue. Yet all these things occur. If humans relied solely on logic, such realities would drive them, literally, crazy. But the human intellect has evolved to be totally comfortable in this environment of contradiction and mystery.

The brain's flexibility in this seemingly chaotic environment has endowed it with unique strengths but also notable weaknesses. For instance, while both the brain and computers have speed and power, their one-of-a-kind processing systems result in dramatically different abilities. The human brain can easily best any supercomputer at recognizing faces, understanding language, or guiding a body's physical movements. Yet, it cannot come close to matching the most basic computer processor's ability to solve complex mathematical equations.[5]

# Part Two: Connectionism

||||||||||||||||||||||||||

After scientists recognized that human intellect was not based on logic, a new theory explaining intelligence, called Connectionism, emerged. Connectionism recognizes the brain as a collection of millions of neurons, each tied to thousands of other neurons that, as a whole, act as the brain's knowledge base. The brain is able to perform as many as two hundred trillion operations in a second, not serially but simultaneously, and this allows vast amounts of knowledge to be brought to bear on a decision all at once.[6]

Because of Connectionism, the human brain can instantly access information from previous experience that seems relevant to the problem at hand. This is how the mind can thrive on imperfect information; it can generalize and fill in missing parts from its large reserves of worldly knowledge, make plausible guesses, and be satisfied with fast, approximate solutions.[7]

This process often masquerades as logical reasoning. Previous experience becomes our substitute for "rational" thought, as the human brain *recognizes* answers to problems rather than deducing them from facts. We gain useful insights instantaneously, but at the cost of making frequent errors.

Human memory cannot help but connect things that seem familiar. Given just a small fragment of information, it instantly amplifies that little piece into a sizable parcel of knowledge.[8] Sometimes it makes mistakes that do not matter; other times the mistakes have consequences. For example, when we walk into an office building and see the lobby lined with green leafy objects sitting in pots, we instantly assume that we are looking at live plants. While it is just as likely we are looking at plastic foliage, the error is inconsequential to us, so we do not need to investigate to see if our assumption is correct.

But what if you are sitting in your kitchen while it is pouring rain outside? Suddenly you feel water dripping from the ceiling. You grab a flashlight and rush into the attic to look for the leak in the roof. After an exhaustive search turns up no leak, you come back down only to discover that an upstairs toilet has overflowed. This time, your immediate connection between the rain outside and the water dripping in your kitchen is much more costly: the drip has turned into a flood. Because of frequent mistakes like these, our decisions often appear to be based on trial and error. But true scientific trial and error involves a conscious, focused effort to answer a particular question; instead our brain is merely making automatic, often sloppy instinctive connections.

Connectionism explains how our instant application of knowledge tricks us into believing that we have an immediate answer. We rarely consider alternative answers, even when we should. Nevertheless, we are able to extend and amplify limited data on the basis of what we know about how the world typically behaves.[9]

Stephen Hoch, of the Wharton School, cites years of psychological experiments that show how efficiently people incorporate new information into existing experience; they can make quick inferences, fill in details, and add meaning to a situation. And as a result, they make much faster decisions. In predictable environments, such Connectionism works very well. But, in unpredictable environments, such as today's increasingly complex global economy, it can cause us to make serious mistakes.[10] The inevitable weakness of this kind of decision-making structure is that humans tend to manufacture patterns, fill in information, and make assumptions that are highly inaccurate or completely untrue.

Jon Miller, CEO of America Online, has seen this phenomenon in action:

> "My experience is that executives try to apply something that they've done previously to the moment. And that can tend to make you not understand the specifics of the situation at hand. Things do change, and unless you are actually looking at the situation itself, you're not seeing it.
>
> In my own way I'm a bit of a contrarian. I'm most comfortable with people who do not do things by rote—they really look at the situation for what it is. One of the big things that get companies in trouble is that they are not intellectually honest, due to personal agendas, vested interests, or muscle memory about the world. That prevents them from assessing situations and seeing things as they really are. I tend to believe there is an answer for anything as long as you look at the reality of things. A leader's challenge is to help people to actually get to the reality of things. From there you can build, you can move forward—not just using accepted wisdom but looking at things for what they really are."

# Part Three: Common Errors of Business Judgment

||||||||||||||||||||||||||

The mind thrives on imperfect data. We can turn nonsense into sense because our brain has been designed for a world where a fast, plausible interpretation is often better than a slow, certain one. Yet the strength of this everyday intelligence carries with it an unexpected liability. The very way our minds have evolved to process information is often the root cause of the most common and most dangerous errors in business judgment. Cornell's J. Edward Russo and Wharton's Paul Schoemaker, in their book *Winning Decisions*, identified the most prevalent of these mistakes.[11] Each can be directly traced to the unique architecture and thought processes of the brain, whose Connectionist structure makes it vulnerable.

## Undue Optimism/Overconfidence

Russo and Schoemaker suggest that the vast majority of executives suffer from what they term "Undue Optimism" or "Overconfidence." This is not a personality trait, such as arrogance or inflated ego. Rather, it refers to the common tendency to subconsciously overestimate how much we know about a particular subject, blinding us to our lack of the crucial information required to render a skilled answer. We tend to make immediate decisions without considering the limitations of the facts that form the basis of our conclusions, so we develop beliefs with unjustified conviction. As a result, we often do not know enough about a problem we are confronting before we've already decided on a solution for it.

It is the brain's Connectionist structure that makes undue optimism such a pervasive problem. The mind naturally focuses on what we know about a situation, to the exclusion of what we do not know. It fails to ask a crucial question: What else do we need to know in order to reach a sound conclusion? Instead, the mind's tendency to make instant connections creates overconfidence that tricks us into believing that our initial assessments are complete.

Rick Lenny, chairman, president, and CEO of the Hershey Company, explains that overconfidence, while common, is not necessarily a result of arrogance:

> "As executives, we often encounter situations where people want to show how 'smart' they are. But not so much in an egotistical sense. I think it's more of a way for people to exert some control over their environment and achieve some level of security. If one can cite numerous facts and show a really good grasp of the data, then this person feels as though they have a bit of 'protective coating.' However, people can be so focused on proving what they know about a topic that they fail to consider what they don't know."

Overconfidence causes decision makers to jump to premature conclusions. When Marijn Dekkers took over leadership of Thermo Electron, he noticed a certain trend. Thermo's core businesses were being run by some of the most brilliant technical minds in the world. But their product-development initiatives tended to be guided by the "novelty" of the technology rather than the market need for a product. Dekkers explains how he went about negating the undue optimism underlying some of his general managers' decisions:

> "They tend to have so much passion for the technology, but they don't critically look at the utility of the technology. It's a blind love. This is understandable: their focus and expertise is in technology. But it's not necessarily in bringing that technology to market. This manifests itself in a variety of ways, such as we *can* make this product ten pounds lighter, therefore we should, regardless of whether the customer wants or needs it."

Dekkers goes on to explain how he countered this blind enthusiasm:

> "The challenge was to get these general managers to temper their knee-jerk enthusiasm for any new technology by questioning whether they had considered the most pertinent issues. So we would ask them for more data relating to the business viability of the idea. For instance, 'Aren't you going to end up with $3 million of obsolete inventory if you introduce a new product?' This got people to include other essential issues in their evaluation of a potential new technology."

By questioning their underlying assumptions, Dekkers used sound reasoning to help his executive team. He not only introduced important new issues for their consideration, but also used skilled questioning to help them to recognize their costly tendency toward incomplete analysis.

# Availability Bias

Executives also frequently suffer from what Russo and Schoemaker term "Availability Bias." They argue that we are inherently prone to assume that the most available information is also the most relevant, even when such conclusions are totally illogical.[12] For instance, the last person who has the boss's ear about a particular issue can often hold an undue influence over his or her final decision. The same is true regarding a lawyer's speech during closing arguments. Undecided juries will tend to focus much more on the statements they heard during a final twenty-minute monologue than on what they witnessed during several weeks of evidence from multiple sources.

This is the brain's equivalent of an optical illusion, a trick similar to the one presented in the well-known drawing of two figures standing on a sloped plain. In the picture, the man in the foreground always appears much larger; yet if we were to measure the two individuals with a ruler, we would discover both to be the same size. In a similar way, information that is close at hand often takes on disproportionate importance.

The most readily available data, because it is immediate and vivid, tricks the mind into thinking that it is central to the issue at hand. Such automatic assumptions can be very misleading, because often the most pertinent data is neither the most obvious nor the most accessible.

A landmark cognition experiment presented in a 1982 paper by Princeton University psychologist and Nobel laureate Daniel Kahneman and Stanford University psychologist Amos Tversky underscores this point.[13] They gave subjects a brief profile about a bank teller named Linda, suggesting that in college she had been an active campaigner against social injustice. The subjects were then asked which was more likely: (a) Linda is a bank teller, or (b) Linda is a bank teller *and* an active feminist. Subjects overwhelmingly chose statement b, even though it was far less likely than statement a.

When the same question was posed as a pure logic test, something quite different happened. For instance, when people were asked, which is more likely to be true, $x$ alone, or $x$ *and* $y$, most people quickly realized that $x$ alone is more likely to be true than $x$ *and* $y$. But even trained statisticians choose the wrong answer when the same equation is posed as a story.

In the Linda scenario, $x$ becomes the certainty we are given—namely, that Linda is a bank teller. And $y$ becomes Linda's possible additional characteristic—that she is an active feminist. Remember, logic dictates that $x$ alone is far more likely than $x$ *plus* a possible $y$. Because we are told something that triggers an association, however (that Linda had been politically active in college), our minds seize upon the available information and assume it is relevant. In fact, however, we are taking two highly suspect leaps in logic: first, that campaigning against social injustice is equated with feminism, and second, that as an adult Linda would maintain an activity she may or may not have participated in during college.

And here again we see how the brain's Connectionist structure causes it to leap to unwarranted conclusions. When confronted with a mathematical equation, we apply analytic skills we have learned. Yet, when we are confronted with problems in real life, instead of analyzing our way to a solution, we feel we *know* the answer. In other words, we make automatic assumptions based on that which is familiar. It is our natural inclination to use the information that is readily at hand, without critically evaluating its relevance. And so we leap to unlikely and unreasonable conclusions. Such flawed assumptions represent one of the most common mistakes in executive judgment.

Jim Williams, a partner at Texas Pacific Group (TPG), is responsible for the senior-level recruitment and hiring at TPG's portfolio companies.

One of the world's largest and most-respected private-equity firms, TPG has a portfolio that includes holdings such as Burger King, Continental Airlines, and J. Crew. They have an impressive track record for turning around underperforming businesses. When Williams talks about Texas Pacific's star leaders, he points to an important common attribute: they are extremely vigilant about digging beneath the surface of information presented to them.

> "Our best CEOs always look skeptically at the data they are given, not just in terms of accuracy, but also in terms of relevance and sufficiency regarding the issues being considered.
>
> These leaders are incisive, insightful, and dogged to get to the bottom of something. They have what I would call a healthy skepticism. I've seen some of our best CEOs get very granular, asking tough questions about the information they have been given, what it means, and what it doesn't mean, and what else they'll still need to know.
>
> This innate curiosity—it's so critical. Our most outstanding CEOs are *incredible investigators;* they ask you a question, they ask another question, and they don't stop. They don't stop until they've gotten to the truth of what they are confronting."

Again, availability bias is not a result of lazy executive behavior. It is a natural tendency of all human beings to make instant associations and magnify information that is presented to them. But these inferences often occur before we've critically evaluated the facts themselves. Without conscious effort to dig further, the most valuable insights often remain hidden.

Jon Miller, America Online's CEO, elaborates:

"So often people come to meetings with information that if taken at face value can be very misleading. My first concern here is always that we get the appropriate facts in the room before we start reaching conclusions. That means checking the data's validity and understanding whether these facts are the most pertinent and are enough to make our decision.

For instance, we have a subscriber base of over 20 million people, and historically AOL has drawn lots of conclusions about this group based upon survey averages and then taken action accordingly. What we discovered, however, was that those averages could be very misleading. That within this enormous subscriber base there were highly diverse, identifiable subgroups. And understanding the differences among the needs of these subgroups is extremely valuable. Just relying on aggregated numbers, as AOL had done in the past, failed to highlight those distinctions.

One example is that we compete in a market with significant price competition. And one of the things we've discussed is should we respond by lowering our price? And if you looked at the aggregated survey numbers, you would get the answer that we should absolutely do that—compete on price. Because our surveys indicate a large percentage of our subscriber base rates price as a concern. However, within this large population you find cohorts of millions of people that are not dissatisfied with AOL's price. Their needs are much more focused on service quality. And just shifting the prices would have taken a lot of money out of our pockets without better satisfying their needs.

But until we began more rigorously analyzing the data and recognizing these subcategories, we could not possibly have gleaned these types of insights. That only came from breaking down the facts, and not continuing our historical tendency to simply render conclusions from the global averages of our subscriber base. *Going beneath the surface-level facts, even though they are indeed the facts, was one of the most useful things we've done here.*"

Jon Miller's experience at AOL highlights the importance of evaluating information for what it can and cannot tell us. Through vigorous questioning and healthy skepticism, the mind's habit for blindly accepting available information can be resisted.

## Frames

One of the most frequently discussed mental habits that influences executive business judgment is the use of "frames," the negative side effects of which are considered to be one of the most crucial and persistent causes of inaccurate analysis. What are frames? They are mental accommodations that allow us to control what information we attend to and, just as important, what we filter out. Because of time constraints in the real world, a completely open mind would be paralyzed if it were forced to consider all possibilities. Instead, we are capable of focusing on only a fraction of the information available to us at any given time. How do we choose what to focus on and what to ignore?

Subconsciously our mind guides us, based upon our past experiences and memories. But the pitfall of relying upon experience and memory is that our minds tilt toward one particular interpretation of reality and away from others. For instance, employers know that, in general, financial compensation is one of the most important concerns of their employees. So when it comes to improving employee satisfaction, they frequently turn to cash bonuses. However, studies have shown that nonmonetary recognition, such as handwritten thank-you notes for a job well done, tend to have a much more powerful and lasting effect on employee satisfaction.[14] When one views worker morale only through the lens of extrinsic, financial needs, one may overlook much more powerful intrinsic, emotional needs.

Creating frames often enables us to anticipate the way things will play out and how people will behave. In some respects, this is very useful, because it allows us to apply our limited experiences to a much broader range of situations or circumstances. But the price we pay for this is a distortion of reality.

Pat Russo, CEO of Lucent Technologies, talks about how executives can be blinded by their own perspectives and experiences:

> "Around here we call it our 'files.' We are all a function of what we have experienced, and that can sometimes limit our thinking regarding what's possible, what's not possible, what will work, and what won't. I've found a great benefit in consciously acknowledging the existence of our own 'files' particularly before we embark upon something really significant.
>
> Take a discussion about a particular emerging market. People will say, 'Well, this is what we've experienced in that market before, and based upon that, this is what I think will happen now.' They'll give you a litany of reasons why a new initiative won't work. This is when it's most crucial to remember how your thinking can be limited by your historical experiences. If you are working on creating something new and different, this can be your biggest handicap. You may be constrained in your thinking and perspective. It's just human nature.
>
> Let me give you an example. Here at Lucent we went through such a dramatic downturn that my team was constantly (and understandably) focusing on reducing, shrinking, restructuring, and exiting businesses in response to the severe declines in the market. So when I started discussions about what we needed to do to 'grow' the business, people just couldn't wrap their minds around it. And that's not surprising, since we'd spent the last two years in reduction mode. So I realized we had a lot of work to do if we were going to drive a major paradigm shift in people's thinking. I didn't want what we could be-

come to be constrained by where we'd been. In this case, it required a real understanding of our own 'file systems.' "

Frames bring with them the illusion of completeness, and it is this illusion, rather than the existence of frames per se, that is the real problem. Because frames exclude information, the world one sees through a frame is never complete; each frame highlights or hides different aspects of a situation. But frames, like stereotypes, are so powerful that they can seem more real than reality itself. They are lenses through which the mind looks at the world, reasons about it, and predicts what will happen next. The cost of seeing clearly through a lens, however, is that some aspects of reality are magnified and others made virtually invisible. This has been referred to as "Frame Blindness." [15]

All too often, managers look out at the world through one mental window and fail to notice other views. They may operate from outdated frames (using a domestic frame when an industry is globalizing, for example) or try to solve a marketing problem by using a sales frame. Worse yet, they may not even realize they are doing so. [16]

Jim Kilts, CEO of Gillette, talks about how shifting his team's mental frames in response to a competitive challenge helped to illuminate an effective countermove:

"The introduction of Schick's four-blade Quattro razor into the market was viewed as a major potential threat to Gillette. People were clamoring to hear how we were going to defend against the $100 million investment Schick had put into this new product offering. During a meeting with my top team, it quickly became clear that we had no immediate ability to address this from a technological standpoint. Our new Mach3 Power vibrating razor was still a number of months away from release. But we knew that there had to be other options. If we couldn't respond to this challenge as a technological problem, we needed to identify a new path of defense.

After much discussion and debate, we reframed the issue as a marketing challenge rather than a technical challenge. We knew we still had an excellent product in our existing Mach3 shaving system. So we created a campaign to redirect attention back to that product. We changed its silver-colored handle to red and added a descriptor to its name, calling it the Mach3 Turbo Champion. We then built a whole marketing program around it to make it exciting to the consumer, and had some of the highest-scoring advertising in the history of the company. Our sales went up 34 percent during that period of defense against the Schick Quattro.

Later, one of the senior executives from Schick that I ran into said, 'You killed us with that little red razor.' It was a great functioning of the team: sales, marketing, technical people, and ad agency coming together to build on the knowledge we have—to say, we don't have any new technical response to this competition, so what we need is to leverage our existing product in a new way. A marketing solution to a technical problem."

Though two windows in a high-rise building may offer expansive views, neither view on its own is complete. Each may offer essential information, but individually they do not allow us to fully understand what is going on outside. By recognizing the particular perspective from which they were initially viewing a problem, Jim Kilts and his team identified alternative viewpoints that had much more bearing on an ultimate solution. The Gillette example demonstrates how the limitations of "frames" can be overcome by certain cognitive skills, such as *using multiple perspectives* or *defining a problem in different ways* in order to come up with creative solutions.

# Pattern Matching

Finally, there are the flaws inherent in "pattern matching." Stephen Hoch discusses the often disastrous tendency of executives to see links and patterns that do not, in fact, exist.[17] The human mind instinctually assumes that the world is causally connected. For instance, no matter how much experience an individual has with games of chance, it is exceptionally hard to grasp that there is no such thing as a "hot hand" in gambling. The mind resists this simple truth because we are naturally wired to look back on the events leading up to a series of winning hands, recognize an apparent pattern, and anticipate a repeat.

The mind has developed a short-cut that simulates how the world works. And nine times out of ten it is right, or at least in the ballpark. But this is only an approximation of our reality. It is hardly a complete understanding of all the circumstances surrounding us at any given moment. When we think about descending a flight of stairs, we don't pay attention to the height of each step. We walk down without thinking about it, because we've performed this task thousands of times before.

If, however, there is some unexpected variation in the height between two steps, we tend not to notice it, and we stumble. This is not a result of lack of coordination. It's simply a result of our minds attempting to navigate our world. If we were to analyze every staircase we came to, we would be paralyzed. Patterns allow our brains to simplify the world into a predictable system, one that approximates how the world works and allows us to function efficiently within it.

It is, in fact, the creation of these cause-and-effect links that makes the world seem less chaotic. But there is a cost to our reliance upon these patterns; our tendency to apply them leaves us vulnerable to massive errors in judgment. For instance, as in gambling, some of the patterns we discern do not truly exist. There actually is no causal link between one roll of the dice and the next. Equally problematic are situations that depart from historical patterns, causing us to anticipate events that will never happen and to be blindsided by others that do.

During the economic boom of the 1990s, stock prices rose dramatically for five years. It was unlike anything that had happened before. But many people failed to secure any profit from their paper gains during this time because they kept or bought more stock, even when prices had dramatically surpassed fundamental corporate valuations. Reliance upon a pattern overcame careful judgment.

And it is this type of reliance on past patterns that can cause a company to miss critical threats to its core business. Jon Miller noticed this happening to America Online:

> "I arrived at AOL in late 2002, at a time when unquestionably the broadband high-speed market was taking off. Astoundingly, AOL was literally still debating whether broadband was actually going to amount to anything. It was extraordinary. These were very capable executives, but because their lens was so much affected by the business they had grown up in, they could not see the situation for what it was.
>
> It was my job to get people in sync with what was going on. I started by presenting them with the data and facts, and asking them, 'If you are wrong, what does that mean? Think about the consequences of that point of view. If you're wrong, what happens to this company?'
>
> You can't change people's understanding of reality overnight. You can't simply walk into a situation where a company has had a single focus for its entire life, and then instantly make it something else altogether. But you can get people to consider the consequences of what they are saying and to think through those consequences. So for me it was helping them follow down the logic of what would happen if AOL could no longer define itself as a dial-up company. What if our histor-

**ical success in that business was no longer relevant, and the world really had changed?"**

The human brain constantly assumes that history repeats itself. But as Jon Miller's example illustrates, allowing historical patterns to dominate your business thinking can be very dangerous. Even if overreliance on patterns does not result in disaster, it can prevent an organization from attaining greater success.

Most great new ideas, once achieved, seem patently obvious in retrospect. We've all been confronted with revolutionary ideas to which we responded, "Why didn't I think of that?" Creativity and invention are the fuel that businesses rely upon to move forward. But our natural attempt to understand the present in terms of our past inhibits us from recognizing new opportunities. It takes a conscious effort to challenge our overreliance on historical patterns. Finding areas for innovation and opportunity requires the ability to see how things have changed, or how they can be done differently.

When Rick Lenny first came on board at the Hershey Company, he set about challenging conventional thinking:

"When I first arrived four years ago, we started implementing a new strategy to reassess the way we viewed each of our brands. For instance, we started discussing our Reese's brand, which is a billion-dollar-a-year franchise at the retail level. The mind-set here was: 'It's Reese's. It's doing well and should continue to do okay.' And that meant growing by low, single digits per year, because that's about what it had done.

So I said to our team, 'Well, let's take a step back and think about what is so inherently powerful about this brand and where can we take it?' This was not about typical brand-building. Nor was it just about challenging the thinking that low growth was good enough. It was more than that. It required really challenging everything that Hershey had been about with this particular brand.

We needed to identify Reese's core strengths and determine if we were leveraging them. So we took a look at the brand. Okay, the Reese's brand is basically a package, two cups. We do something different at Halloween and something at Easter, and so on. It was somewhat 'uni-dimensional' in its benefit and delivery. So we asked ourselves, 'What can we do in convenience or variety? What can we do in "better for you"? How can we extend into high-growth segments such as snacking and nutrition bars?'

Then we started thinking past the brand to the key ingredients. We said, 'Well, it has chocolate and peanut butter—great idea for a cookie. Let's take it on multiple dimensions as opposed to repetitively going down the same path we had before.'

Two years later we've come out with unbelievable product and equity extensions, and by-and-large Reese's has been our fastest-growing brand. And the breakthrough was that we needed to look at it through the other end of the telescope. It required a lot of people to think *and* act differently.

It may not be as exciting as some divestiture or acquisition, but this new perspective with Reese's has enabled us to think more broadly across the organization. And we've been able to apply this critical type of thinking and really expand it to many other areas of the company well beyond 'brand marketing.'

If we had not done that with Reese's, and unshackled our thinking about something that was so basic in everyone's minds—one of the most powerful brands in the company—we might not have made some of these other advances. We've now moved into cookies, nutrition bars, and, with our acquisition of Mauna Loa, the macadamia snack nut business."

Rick Lenny's comments highlight how looking at historical patterns can cause our thinking to stagnate. Pressing to understand what has changed, what can change, and what new opportunities are presenting themselves is something leaders must be able to do. Yet, our brains have trained us to recognize patterns all around us. This gives us a sense of security, the feeling that what is happening is something we've already seen before. But in business, we must battle against this automatic, habitual tendency because it can pose a serious obstacle to innovative thinking, and it can trick us into seeing patterns that don't exist. An executive must learn to slough off the unquestioned acceptance of an emerging pattern. And by retraining the mind—questioning the patterns—we can make our decisions more reliable.

Jim Kilts describes his response to this challenge:

"I start to feel very uncomfortable when we seem to be moving blindly in a tried-and-true direction. People can too easily become dependent on what they already know. So sometimes I'll throw out an outlandish idea to get people thinking. It's a good way to get people going, especially when they are just relying on what they've always done in the past. So I get them to defend their positions, and sometimes you need to say something outlandish to shake up an organization and get people thinking critically."

The well-documented practice managers have of acting without thinking is due to the evolutionary advantage provided to the human brain by applying knowledge to instantly recognize solutions to problems. We have no instinctive need to apply skilled reasoning, since during evolutionary conditions, sharp analysis was not useful. In fact, careful consideration could consume precious seconds, thereby threatening survival, making instant, approximate solutions far more valuable.

It is because of this evolutionary compromise that business leaders generally lack Executive Intelligence. They don't have a deficiency; they simply are behaving more in line with natural human tendencies. This is precisely why Executive Intelligence is so hard to find, and why, in many ways, the aptitudes composing Executive Intelligence are quite unnatural.

But the rarity of Executive Intelligence makes it all the more important that we embark on a focused pursuit of this valuable resource. Just as geologists, when prospecting, have come to know the characteristics that signal the presence of precious metals below the surface, it is necessary for us to be able to spot the telltale signs of Executive Intelligence. Presently, the only measures designed to assess cognitive abilities of any kind are IQ tests. So a closer examination of these tests and how they work is a logical place to start.

# CHAPTER 7 SUMMARY

||||||||||||||||||||||||||

- The way our minds process information leads us to draw unwarranted conclusions and take immediate action without thinking first. This comes as the result of the way our brains have evolved over millions of years.

- In today's modern business environment, our mind's predilection for drawing instant conclusions and leaping into action is often more of a hindrance than a help.

- The human mind has no inherent system of logic. In fact, the human brain is consistently, systematically *illogical*.

- "Connectionism" causes the human brain to instantly access information from previous experience that seems relevant to the problem at hand, and this process often masquerades as logical reasoning.

- *Undue Optimism, Availability Bias, Pattern Matching,* and *Frames* are some of the most common causes of poor decisions, and each comes as a direct result of the brain's unique "Connectionist" architecture.

- One of the main reasons Executive Intelligence is so rare is that the aptitudes composing it are contrary to the natural tendencies of the human brain.

# SECTION III:

# INTELLIGENCE IS THE KEY

# CHAPTER 8

# Part One: Beyond Academic Intelligence

As we've discussed, a particular set of cognitive abilities differentiates star executives from their peers, but until now, the only cognitive skills that could be measured were those that were originally identified to predict the academic performance of schoolchildren. These are the skills commonly assessed by traditional IQ tests, and though these instruments do, to some extent, predict work performance, they assess only a fraction of the total number of cognitive abilities that exist. And, more important, the aptitudes measured by traditional IQ tests are not necessarily the ones most crucial to business success.

Historically, we've had to rely upon IQ measures to sort executive candidates—either through formal testing or by hiring individuals with elite degrees—because these were the only indicators that existed. In other words, we've been relying on academic aptitude to predict work intelligence. To some extent this has been appropriate, since the cognitive skills necessary for academic performance overlap somewhat with those required for executive work.

However, as Jim Kilts of Gillette explains, more than just academic thinking skills are necessary:

"Many of the top business leaders have attended elite academic institutions, and this education can serve as a good foundation—[developing] the ability to think critically and understand concepts. So a doctorate can be an indication of intellectual horsepower. But in a business setting you must be able to not only generate ideas but translate those ideas into results. That is the hardest thing and requires abilities that go beyond academic skills."

As Kilts points out, the additional abilities that star business performers possess are not the same as those that determine success in academics. Clearly, we must create a measure that is specific to managerial work. The solution seems simple, but until the cognitive skills that comprise Executive Intelligence had been identified, it was not possible to create such a measure. With the recognition of the cognitive skills essential to business leadership, we can finally set about creating such a test. The first step in that process is to understand how intelligence tests are created.

# Part Two: How Intelligence Measures Are Created

|||||||||||||||||||||||||||

Cognitive abilities, like all psychological traits, are invisible. To create measures of intelligence, researchers have to choose observable qualities that signal the presence of underlying aptitudes. In other words, since we cannot actually see a cognitive ability, we have to find some outward sign of its existence. It is like detecting the wind by observing wheat bending in a field. Although we cannot physically see a person's intelligence, we can measure its presence and strength by observing activities that require it.

This task is complicated by the fact that there is little agreement about what specific activities denote intelligence. In fact, there still exists no universally accepted definition of this concept. It turns out that defining intelligence has been a contentious, intensely debated topic ever since scientists became interested in the subject.

When IQ testing first came into widespread use, the lack of consensus was an acknowledged problem. One of the original creators of IQ tests, Harvard University psychologist Edwin Boring, when pressed for his definition, responded, "Intelligence is what intelligence tests measure."[1]

Psychologists have resorted to surveying experts in an effort to produce some agreement on the subject. The first and most famous study was published in the *Journal of Educational Psychology* in 1921. Responses ranged from "sensation, perception, association, memory, imagination, discrimination, judgment, and reasoning," to "the capacity to acquire capacity."[2] These surveys of expert opinion continue to be circulated today, but still little agreement has been achieved.

As a result, the choice of abilities to be included in an intelligence measure is left to the creator of the test and are, therefore, highly subjective. IQ tests tend to be designed to detect a combination of abilities that *the creator* of the test believes display intelligence.

And that is how IQ tests have become so misleading. They are referred to as "intelligence" assessments, implying a complete measure of this concept. But a virtually unlimited range of cognitive abilities could be considered for inclusion. Any instrument claiming to be a global measure is inevitably inadequate.

These tests evaluate candidates' capacities in a very narrow range of activities; the tests are relevant only to the degree that the specific skills they measure are the same skills that will be called for later. For instance, if you are trying to assess how someone will perform in a math class, having him or her solve word-analogy problems will yield scores far less predictive than will arithmetic problem-solving questions.

There is *some* overlap between these activities; the type of overarching ability that makes someone good at math also helps in verbal subjects. So predicting someone's math aptitude from their score on a verbal test would be more accurate than, say, basing it on how fast they can run a mile. But using verbal scores is significantly less accurate than using math scores to predict performance in mathematics. The inaccuracy inherent in any IQ measure is largely determined by how irrelevant or incomplete the skills measured are with regard to the application for which these scores are being used.

In the popular movie *Rain Man*, Dustin Hoffman's character, Raymond Babbitt, suffered from autism. Although he displayed severe limitations when it came to the most basic tasks (like confusing hot and cold water when running a bath), he was incredibly gifted at determining numerical sequences. If one were to define intelligence as one's ability to perform that particular mathematical task, Raymond would be considered a genius. Yet a more reasonable view of his capabilities would classify him as a savant, a person with outstanding skills within a very narrow range of activities.

The *Rain Man* example shows that the genius label has as much to do with the test maker's selection of cognitive skills as it does with the abilities of the individual being tested. When it comes to business, the failure to build an intelligence measure that focuses on specific relevant skills has created somewhat of a quandary. Companies are told to rely upon intelligence to judge the quality of a candidate, yet the measures available were not constructed for that purpose.

Most of us have had experience with individuals who are considered "geniuses" from an IQ perspective yet who lack some of the most basic skills of effective executives, such as differentiating crucial priorities from more secondary concerns, or recognizing how a particular statement would be unnecessarily offensive to colleagues.

To understand and correct the limitations of current intelligence tests, it is important to understand how they have evolved along with the changing notions about what it means to be smart.

# Part Three: The Changing Notions of Intelligence

||||||||||||||||||||||||||

The first "intelligence tests" were created in 1883 by Sir Francis Galton, who theorized that two core qualities characterized human intelligence: energy and sensitivity to stimuli.[3] Galton, a renowned scientist and one of the world's first psychologists, observed that intellectually capable people appeared to have a higher capacity for labor. Therefore, he presumed that individuals who possessed more energy—and who consequently could labor longer—must be smarter. Galton also believed that individuals with higher intelligence were more sensitive to physical stimuli. In his view, they had superior physical dexterity and a heightened awareness of the surrounding physical environment.

Galton's definition of intelligence was grounded in physical attributes and had clearly been influenced by the theories of evolution and competitive survival introduced by his cousin Charles Darwin.[4] For Galton, intelligence was represented by observable physical qualities that promoted the survival of one individual over another. He believed that intelligence was grounded, not in the academic criteria that are central to today's tests, but in those abilities that gave one person an advantage over another in the natural struggle for survival.

To measure intelligence, Galton would put subjects through a battery of tests, including hearing measurements and physical challenges, that determined the speed of a subject's reflexes and the range of his or her senses. Between 1884 and 1890 people curious to test their abilities visited Galton at the South Kensington Museum in London and paid to have their intelligence measured.[5] Although Galton was the first to attempt a measure of human intelligence, his theory was never widely accepted and his methods remained nothing more than an amusing footnote in history.

Subsequent intelligence tests were influenced less by evolutionary theory than by the need to determine a child's academic potential. The cognitive ability tests we recognize today originated with the minister of public instruction in Paris, who, in 1904, created a commission to identify students who were struggling academically because of their mental defects. He wanted to ensure that children were sent to classes for the mentally retarded *only* if they could not profit from ordinary instruction. In the fall of 1904, Alfred Binet was appointed to this commission.[6]

Alfred Binet and his colleague Theodore Simon created a test to suit the education minister's needs. They felt that a child's academic potential could be best measured using problem-solving tests containing material of the kind he or she would confront in school. Binet's concepts were soon imported to the United States, where Stanford University's Lewis Terman, a professor of psychology, created the Stanford-Binet test, whose current version is still a leader in the intelligence-testing market.[7]

These tests focused on vocabulary and arithmetic skills, as well as mechanical and spatial reasoning (topics taught in school), and they required candidates to solve problems in a written, multiple-choice format also common in academic settings. Over time, these tests have been shown to be exceptional predictors of school success, enabling administrators to distinguish exceptionally gifted students or severely handicapped students and place them into environments well suited to their abilities. But society's desire to categorize people soon led to the use of IQ tests outside of the scope for which they were originally intended.

# Part Four: IQ Tests and Managerial Work

|||||||||||||||||||||||||

During World War I, American psychologists, eager to contribute to the war effort, adapted Binet's intelligence tests for the U.S. Army as an inexpensive way to differentiate among large numbers of recruits.[8] This was the first large-scale use of intelligence testing on a group of adults, and it suggested that these school-based tests could predict performance in nonacademic situations.

Consequently, the high-profile role psychologists played in the job assignment of recruits created tremendous interest in the private sector. It was during this time that the *Journal of Applied Psychology,* the oldest and most prestigious journal in the field of industrial psychology, began publication, starting with a series of articles about real-world applications of intelligence testing.

After World War I several research institutes were founded in an effort to broaden the benefits of psychological testing. One of these, the Psychological Corporation, established by psychologist James Cattell, still exists today as one of the largest publishers of psychological tests for employee selection. By the 1950s, the use of intelligence testing by employers had become commonplace.

Since then, IQ testing has become one of the most widely applied and extensively researched of all psychological tools. Although its predictive validity is highest for its original purpose—school success—IQ has proven to be a powerful predictor of performance for virtually any occupation.[9]

In 1998, two of the most respected researchers in assessment methodologies, Professors Frank Schmidt of the University of Iowa and John Hunter of Michigan State University, published in the American Psychological Association's *Psychological Bulletin* a landmark study analyzing over eighty-five years of research findings. They compared the predictive validity of all major assessment methodologies and declared that IQ is a measure that should be included when hiring virtually any employee.[10] In a 2004 follow-up study, Schmidt and Hunter combined the results of 515 independent studies involving over 100,000 employees. They declared that cognitive ability tests predict occupational performance "better than any other ability, trait, or disposition, and better than job experience."[11]

Further, research has proven that as job complexity increases, so does the predictive validity of IQ. This finding has been borne out repeatedly. For instance, in a large-scale study in 1984 conducted by Professor John Hunter and Ronda Hunter, they combined the results of 425 independent validity studies involving over 32,000 employees.[12] They found that for less complex jobs such as farmhand or laborer, IQ explained about 5 percent of the variance in performance. But for upper-management positions, IQ explained 34 percent. Similar results were reported again in a 2003 study published in the *Journal of Applied Psychology*, combining the results of 138 independent studies involving over 19,000 employees.[13]

As can be seen from the graph, IQ testing is at least as effective as competency interviews (the most common assessment methodology used today for hiring and promotion) as a means to predict managerial success. What's more, IQ tests are approximately ten times as powerful as personality tests. Such results demonstrate the enormous relevance that IQ has to managerial work performance, despite the fact that IQ tests are geared to academic subjects. So, what makes them so predictive?

# PREDICTIVE POWER OF IQ TESTS
# VERSUS OTHER ASSESSMENT INSTRUMENTS*

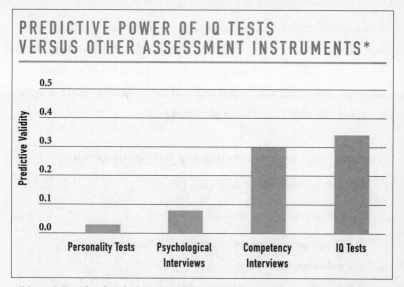

*Murray R. Barrick and Michael K. Mount, "The Big Five Personality Dimensions and Job Perfor-
mance: A Meta-analysis," *Personnel Psychology*, 44, no. 1, (Spring 1991): 1–26; Michael McDaniel,
Deborah Whetzel, Frank Schmidt, and Steven Maurer, "The Validity of Employment Interviews: A
comprehensive Review and Meta-analysis," *Journal of Applied Psychology*, 79 (1994): 599–616;
Stephan Motowidlo, Gary W. Carter, Marvin Dunnette, and Nancy Tippins, "Studies of the Structured Behavioral Interview," *Journal of Applied Psychology*, 77 (no. 5) (October 1992): 571–587.

It turns out that some of the underlying thinking skills so crucial to
executive performance are indeed measured by these tests. Consider this
sample question adapted from a commonly used IQ test that is intended
to evaluate logical inference skills:

Assume the first two statements are true. Is the final one:

(1) True, (2) False, (3) Not certain?

The boy plays baseball.

All baseball players wear hats.

The boy wears a hat.

If we know that the boy plays baseball, and that people who play baseball wear hats, then we can safely make the inference that this boy wears a hat. Answer: True. This sort of reasoning is not unlike the kind that managers must make all the time. Let's rework the above question to make it more obviously related to business decision-making.

> Assume the first two statements are true. Is the final one also true?
>
> ABC company always ships using UPC.
>
> UPC always delivers to us within two days.
>
> Therefore, we should receive the order we just placed with ABC within two days.

Again, with sound reasoning one can conclude that your assumption is indeed true. This is an example of how the reasoning skills measured by certain IQ question types (drawing logical inference) have relevance to managerial responsibilities. But there are also skills measured by IQ tests that have almost no relevance to managerial work, such as:

> Choose the answer that most nearly means the same as the underlined word.
>
> Pertinacious refers to:
>
> (1) Obstinate
>
> (2) Credulous
>
> (3) Prolix
>
> (4) Synoptic

The ability to answer this question is almost purely dependent on one's vocabulary. So if one recognizes the meaning of *pertinacious* as "stubbornly unyielding," one easily picks *(1) Obstinate* as the answer to the question. But individuals with genius levels of vocabulary have no meaningful advantage as managers because such proficiencies have little to do with their professional responsibilities. To the degree that IQ questions reward skills that are less relevant to executive work (such as breadth of vocabulary), the test scores become less predictive.

Although IQ testing assesses a mix of skills, some that are relevant to managerial work and some that are less so, overall these instruments are unquestionably powerful indicators of executive aptitudes. So why isn't IQ testing widely used as a way of identifying top talent? Unfortunately, these tests also carry with them serious shortcomings that inhibit their widespread use with managerial populations. While some of the problems with IQ tests are very real, they have led to a bias against any kind of intelligence testing. This in turn has profoundly hurt businesses' ability to recognize true managerial talent.

# Part Five: Creating an Appropriate Executive IQ Test

|||||||||||||||||||||||||

Given the predictive power of IQ testing, it may seem strange that it is rarely included in an executive assessment. Yet for a number of reasons these tests are perceived as being unfair and irrelevant. As a consequence, executives are very reluctant to take them, and businesses are somewhat afraid to administer them. In other words, despite the incontrovertible predictive value of cognitive-ability testing, it has been discarded because of its imperfections.

As was discussed previously, one obvious obstacle to the use of IQ tests is the perceived irrelevance of the skills they measure. Take the Adult Wechsler IQ test, for instance—the most popular IQ test in use today.[14] This instrument measures language skills through vocabulary and word analogies, assesses math skills using arithmetic questions, and tests spatial reasoning skills using block-arrangement exercises. Obviously, the majority of test questions appear to measure skills too remote from actual executive work.

Problems involving arithmetic, spatial reasoning, or vocabulary are rarely encountered in the course of an executive's decision-making responsibilities, and the vast majority of executives have enough rudimentary skills in these areas to do their jobs well. An unusually broad vocabulary or exceptionally quick mathematical aptitude is unlikely to lead to superior leadership performance. Using these subjects to differentiate among managerial applicants creates a feeling of unfairness. To avoid this flaw, an assessment must utilize subject-relevant questions. Instead of measuring arithmetic skills, for instance, it could focus on skills such as evaluating the quality of data or identifying sound logistical solutions.

Another obstacle to using academic intelligence tests in a business setting is the perceived irrelevance of the testing format. Business executives rarely confront problems in the manner that IQ tests present them, namely, in a multiple-choice format that requires the selection of only one right answer. In business, problems are almost never so well defined, and they generally have all kinds of potential solutions. IQ test questions fail to assess the practical, on-your-feet thinking skills you need in business.

As a result of the deficiencies of the IQ test question formats, the most noteworthy accomplishments of some high-IQ individuals may well be their test scores.[15] So can this problem be corrected? The most obvious solution would be to present intelligence measures in a format that requires immediate verbal responses to questions that have more than one good answer. This format most closely emulates the real business environment and would give the test credibility.

Another reason that IQ measures are not widely used in business is their vulnerability to charges of racial bias. Minority groups have consistently performed worse than Caucasians on such measures. It is likely that these differences in IQ scores (because of the test questions' heavy reliance upon academic subjects) are merely a reflection of the lesser educational opportunities afforded to these groups. An appropriate measure of business intelligence must rely less on educational training and more on a candidate's capacity to perform tasks that are directly involved in managerial decision-making.

A final important impediment to the adoption of IQ testing is that people's scores drop noticeably as they get older. But no reputable psychologist would suggest that people become less intelligent as they age. More likely, they simply grow less skilled at solving academic-type problems because they are further removed from their formal educational training. Many commonly used IQ tests now incorporate an age-related scoring correction to address this problem.[16] Even so, these age-related decreases in IQ scores are often used to support the argument that these tests are inappropriate for the older workers who populate the executive ranks. By creating a business-intelligence measure that tests work-related decision-making skills, age discrimination issues could be effectively eliminated.

These shortcomings have made IQ tests largely unacceptable in today's workplace, resulting in an unmet need for businesses. Organizations know that intelligence matters, yet they have been given no appropriate means for differentiating among their candidates. It is into this vacuum that alternative, broader definitions of intelligence have crept. Of these, none has had more impact on current executive-assessment practices than the concept of emotional intelligence.

# CHAPTER 8 SUMMARY

||||||||||||||||||||||||

- There are skills beyond those necessary for academic success that determine executive effectiveness.

- Traditional IQ measures fail to assess many of the cognitive skills that star business performers possess.

- No universally accepted definition of intelligence exists.

- IQ tests are designed to detect a combination of abilities that *the creator* of the test believes displays intelligence.

- Although their predictive validity is highest for their original purpose—predicting school success—IQ measures have been proven to be a powerful predictor of performance in virtually any occupation.

- Though highly predictive, these tests have serious shortcomings that have almost completely eliminated their use with senior managerial populations.

# CHAPTER 9

## Part One:
## Taking a Wrong Turn

The term *emotional intelligence* first appeared in a 1966 German article entitled "Emotional Intelligence and Emancipation," by Hanscarl Leuner.[1] A research psychologist, Leuner hypothesized that adult women who reject their social roles do so because of their low emotional intelligence. Though he gave no clear definition or measure of his concept, he theorized that his clients were having difficulties understanding and regulating their own emotions because of their premature separation from their mothers. His treatment for the women in his case studies combined administration of the hallucinogenic drug LSD with psychotherapy.

A subsequent reference to emotional intelligence appeared in 1985, in an unpublished dissertation by an English doctoral student named Wayne Payne. He described emotional intelligence as a type of core intelligence in which: "Facts, meanings, truths, relationships, etc., are those that exist in the realm of emotion. Thus, feelings are facts." Payne advocated the cultivation of emotional intelligence in children through the use of therapy and various school activities. These, he noted, were ideal opportunities to help people learn ways to express their emotions more freely.[2]

But emotional intelligence did not receive widespread attention until the publication of Rutgers University professor Daniel Goleman's 1995 book *Emotional Intelligence,* which became a nationwide best seller. He has since published numerous articles in *Harvard Business Review* advising leaders on the importance of his theory and its relevance to their success. Goleman defines *emotional intelligence* as a unique ability characterized by behaviors that include high motivation or drive, strong impulse control, empathy for other people, and a hopeful outlook.[3]

Over time, Goleman's concept of emotional intelligence has had a profound effect on the field of executive assessment. It is hard to find another individual psychologist who has had a broader impact on current executive-evaluation practices. His influence has made it common practice to screen executives for their emotional intelligence, and virtually all major executive search firms include some measure of his theory in their assessment of candidates. Goleman has, through his highly engaging writing style, hammered away at the notion that verbal and math problems should remain the ultimate measures of intelligence. His call for a reexamination of our school-based definition of intelligence has struck a powerful chord both in business circles and with the general public.

Millions of people whose futures had been affected by poor standardized test scores welcomed Goleman's voice for change. Corporate leaders who'd had personal experience with academically brilliant individuals who were less than competent leaders embraced Goleman's concepts, in the hope of finding a better way to identify the star talent they so desperately sought. Goleman deserves credit for vastly increasing popular understanding of the complexity of human intelligence and forcing us to expand our notion of what it means to be smart.

Yet, rarely has a psychological concept that was so readily accepted and so widely applied to business received such scathing criticism in management-science literature. Mainstream researchers' central concern is that emotional intelligence has been prematurely declared to predict work performance, without any empirical evidence to support the contention. A review of the research that has been done on this topic reveals these criticisms to be well founded.

To date, despite the efforts of a multitude of credible research scientists, not one published study has shown emotional intelligence to predict performance above and beyond what could already be explained by other commonly applied and long established measures.[4]

In 2003, two of the most respected and widely published researchers in emotional intelligence, Yale University professor Peter Salovey and University of California–Irvine professor David Pizarro, wrote an article titled "The Value of Emotional Intelligence," in which they summarized the current state of inquiry on this subject.[5]

They pointed out the persistent lack of empirical evidence to show that emotional intelligence can predict work performance, and warned that unsubstantiated assertions about the concept only serve to increase skepticism toward the theory as a whole. They also acknowledged that while there is still no established test of these traits for employee screening, emotional intelligence does provide a useful framework for future research into an important but neglected topic.

Why has it been so hard to prove the value of one of the most popular theories of the last decade? The problem is that the behaviors that have been widely cited as indicators of emotional intelligence have long been recognized as personality traits, tending more toward behavioral preferences than actual aptitudes.

In an article published in the 2000 edition of *Handbook of Intelligence,* psychology Professors Richard Mayer of University of California–Santa Barbara and Peter Salovey of Yale University, and consultant David Caruso of Work-Life Strategies, warned that emotional control, achievement drive, empathy, and positive outlook (all cited as being part of emotional intelligence) are each included within the most commonly used models of personality. They concluded that assessments based on these characteristics will yield little information beyond that offered by readily available personality inventories.[6]

Empirical studies have supported their observation. The Emotional Quotient Inventory (EQ-i), developed by Reuven Bar-On, was the first commercially available and comprehensive measure of emotional intelligence. Independent evaluations of the test showed it to be so highly correlated with personality traits such as conscientiousness, sociability, and empathy that reviewers have declared the EQ-i to be simply a measure of these traits, which have been under investigation for decades.[7]

What's more, personality traits and intelligence—although both widely accepted as important psychological phenomena—have never been shown to have much of a relationship with one another.[8] For instance, bright people have all sorts of personalities. Some are highly aggressive and forceful, while others take a more "laid-back" attitude. A personality type is in no way indicative of how smart a person is, and when it comes to predicting work performance, personality assessments can hardly be considered a substitute for cognitive ability tests.

In 1991, University of Iowa professors Murray Barrick and Michael Mount published the most widely cited study regarding the power of personality to predict work performance and analyzed the empirical research on this topic. For a pool of nearly 24,000 individuals, personality attributes explained only 4 percent of the variance in employee performance ratings.[9] In comparison, IQ, the most commonly used measure of intelligence, accounted for over 30 percent, nearly ten times the predictive power of personality.[10] Emotional intelligence's reliance upon personality traits at its core will always severely limit its predictive power.

Yet regardless of its limitations, it's important to recognize why emotional intelligence has gained so much traction. In part, it is because of the vacuum created by the absence of an appropriate means for understanding and measuring intelligence among executives. The shift away from traditional academic definitions of intelligence has allowed the concept of intelligence to be reintroduced without the distasteful elements of IQ measures. But the substitution of personality for intelligence has distracted observers from the undeniable truth that cognitive ability is one of the most prominent determining factors in executive performance.

Unfortunately, the focus on personality traits as a means for evaluating executives is a problem that has existed in management science for decades. It is an ongoing misconception—a terribly misguided one—that personality and style are key indicators of performance. Let's take a look at another leadership theory dominated by personality: the charismatic-leadership movement, whose influence peaked in the late 1990s.

# Part Two: The Charisma Trap

||||||||||||||||||||||||

The theory of charismatic leadership was first conceived by German sociologist Max Weber during the early 1900s. He described the charismatic leader as "set apart from ordinary men and treated as endowed with . . . exceptional powers and qualities . . . which are not accessible to the ordinary person but are regarded as of divine origin or as exemplary, and on the basis of them the individual concerned is treated as a leader." [11]

To Weber, charismatic leaders were those capable of bringing dramatic change and transformation. He described charisma as "a certain quality of an individual personality." [12] Times of great change or upheaval tend to support the emergence of such personalities, because people seek an authority figure to guide them. For this reason, charismatic leaders are created more by circumstances than by their talents.

Weber points out that charismatic authority is very much dependent on success. When charismatic leaders prevail, their strong personalities are seen as responsible for their success and are seen as a type of talent. Yet, in times of failure the aura surrounding charismatic leaders quickly disappears. [13] This is not surprising, since such failures reveal that many of these individuals lack vital substantive skills.

While charismatic leadership was widely studied by sociologists and political scientists during the 1960s, organizational researchers did not embrace it widely until the late 1980s and '90s. The management scientists promoting this theory described personal charisma as a core determinant of effectiveness. The best leadership, they contended, resulted from the capacity to make exciting and compelling speeches, to articulate extraordinary visions regarding an organization's future, and to take bold symbolic actions that aroused strong emotions and identification in their followers.[14]

Rakesh Khurana, professor of organizational behavior at Harvard Business School, explained the widespread popularity of this concept in his 2002 book, *Searching for a Corporate Savior*. Khurana observed, "The charismatic leader is prized for the ability to inspire and motivate employees and instill confidence in analysts and investors." Yet, as Khurana's research showed, these qualities were often emphasized at the expense of more substantive drivers of executive success. He concluded, "Strategic, political, and other merely managerial skills are discounted as pedestrian and boring, or simply ignored as irrelevant."[15]

So many of the corporate failures of the 1990s, Khurana points out, were due to the hiring of leaders simply because of their charisma rather than their actual skills. He lists several examples of serious failures caused by corporate boards' hiring of dramatic, savior-type personalities rather than carefully evaluating who might really be the most skilled people available for the job.

Pat Russo, CEO of Lucent Technologies, distinguishes personality from capability:

> "Charisma, 'presence'—they are nice to have. But in the end it's one's capability, competence, and leadership that get results. You can have all the charisma in the world, but if you are not effectively leading, managing, and getting results, it won't matter. All the greatest 'claims' mean nothing if you can't ultimately deliver on them. The future will always arrive and reveal whether what you've promised came true."

Jon Miller of AOL takes Russo's distinction between competence and charisma one step further. He explains how charismatic leaders often fail to focus on what is most important to the survival of an organization. As Jon Miller explains:

> "A charismatic style has nothing to do with serving your market and customer more effectively. You have to determine logically what the market requires and the customer needs and how you can build around that. In contrast, the type of organization a charismatic leader builds is centered around them, not the customer."

As Miller points out, charismatic leaders can actually get in the way of building an effective organization. And even though in recent years charismatic leadership has largely been debunked,[16] its legacy remains. The overemphasis on personality and style with regards to executive performance continues unabated. And until we see how relevant and irrelevant criteria are blended in executive evaluations, we cannot hope to untangle this mess.

# Part Three: A Cult of Personality

||||||||||||||||||||||||

Even before the emergence of charismatic-leadership theories or the popularized notion of emotional intelligence, there was an overemphasis on the importance of personality in executive performance.

Leaders with magnetic personalities have a tremendous advantage over more humble or shy executives. Hiring for senior positions generally involves little more than a few conversations with a candidate, and promotions are often overly influenced by characteristics such as charm, likability, and social polish. In all of these situations, style often overwhelms substance.

Yet, as Jim Kilts of Gillette explains, the best executives often have understated personalities, and if they were to be judged by style standards alone, their exceptional talents would be overlooked:

> "Take Doug Conant, the CEO at Campbell Soup. Doug is very thoughtful, understated, self-deprecating, and humble. To some extent, he has an understated personality. He's got charisma, but he doesn't exude it every day. But what a tremendous leader. He takes tough situations and is able to work his way through them. He's got the right answers."

In fact, managers can possess a wide range of behavioral styles and still be equally effective. For instance, although interpersonal warmth is commonly viewed as a positive personality trait, lack of this quality does not significantly inhibit an individual's managerial performance. As with all personality traits, as long as an individual falls within a fairly wide range of what is considered normal behavior, these attributes play a very minor role in how well an executive does his or her job.

Personality is not a differentiator of star talent, and when it is used for that purpose, it becomes a dangerous distraction. University of Chicago psychologist Mihaly Csikszentmihalyi conducted numerous in-depth investigations of the world's most accomplished individuals and found that they did not share any particular set of personality traits.[17]

In his examination of the most ingenious people in human history— corporate leaders, scientists, political leaders, and artists—no common pattern emerged with regard to their styles. The renowned painter Raphael, for instance, was extremely optimistic and extroverted; on the other hand, a fellow celebrated artist who was his contemporary, Michelangelo, was exceedingly negative and introverted. To look to personality as an indicator of their excellence would be fruitless.

Csikszentmihalyi punctuated his findings with a quote from John Reed, the CEO of Citicorp, who said, "I tend to know the guys who run the top fifty, one hundred companies in the country and there's quite a range . . . there's no consistency in style and approach, personality, and so forth. There is not a consistent norm with regard to anything other than business performance."[18]

Consider the dramatic style differences between two extraordinary CEO performers in the pharmaceutical industry. Both were brought in to turn around underperforming companies, and both have been recognized for their dramatic successes in doing so.

Fred Hassan, the current CEO of Schering Plough and former CEO of Pharmacia-Upjohn, is known for his highly empathetic style. Ken Banta, Schering's head of Strategic Communications, notes, "Everyone that works with Fred feels an easy personal connection to him." During

Hassan's six-year tenure at Pharmacia, he engineered a tenfold increase in the market capitalization of the company, which by 2002 culminated in the sale of Pharmacia to Pfizer Inc. for over $60 billion.

Thomas Ebeling engineered a similarly impressive turnaround at Novartis Pharma. In 2000, Ebeling was promoted to be that company's CEO and has been widely credited for turning the sluggish unit into an extremely formidable competitor. By 2001, *Forbes* magazine noted, "Novartis suddenly is outmaneuvering heavyweights like Merck."[19]

Like Fred Hassan's, Ebeling's performance in turning around a struggling pharmaceutical company has been extraordinary. Yet the two men's interpersonal styles could not be more different. Ebeling, an amateur boxer, has a much tougher veneer.[20] Ebeling stresses that good interpersonal relations with his people are essential, and he works hard to maintain them. But, he counsels:

> "There are some occasions when I must be demanding of my team. In those instances it's because I feel it is my responsibility to teach them toughness when dealing with competitors and negotiators. I believe that this is essential in order to help them become better managers in a highly competitive environment.
>
> I love the critical banter with them. I critique and challenge them and expect them to know their facts. We focus together on the issues at hand, and I strive for creative, sharp thinking. Adding this dialogue to an environment is very useful, particularly when you are trying to change organizational practices or habits."

Obviously these two men possess very different personalities. So, if personality was not the decisive factor in their respective successes, what was?

When you talk to them about how they engineered their remarkable corporate turnarounds, the marked differences in their personalities fade in contrast to the remarkable similarities of their thinking. When Hassan, for example, came in as CEO of Pharmacia, he had an aging product line and a pipeline of new drugs with supposedly narrow market potential. He immediately set about redefining the market for Pharmacia's new drugs.

For instance, Detrol, one of Pharmacia's upcoming releases at the time, was being developed for the treatment of urinary incontinence. This condition was fairly rare, limiting the drug's potential market to $100–$200 million a year. Hassan gave vigorous support to an initiative reexamining the previous assumption that the drug was only useful for such a narrow problem. This reexamination led the team to realize that although it was not yet a well-defined medical condition, far more people suffered from a more prevalent form of incontinence, a condition termed "overactive bladder." Detrol was found to be effective in treating this more prevalent malady.

As Hassan elaborates:

"When I got to Pharmacia, I saw a company that was shrinking. We were down to one sales division in primary care. We had lost our confidence and lost our way. Our visions for Detrol, Xalatan (for glaucoma), and Camptosar (for colon cancer) were all too narrow—in the $200 million range. We saw the potential in these new treatments. We had to explain in a substantive way how these treatments were going to transform the success of the company. For instance, there was no market and no category for overactive bladder, there was no medical term. It was only called 'urinary incontinence,' which is a very narrow market. We developed a fresh category, 'overactive bladder.' While urinary incontinence had been seen as a serious but unusual condition, we set about broadening how this condition was understood. We expanded the category from only a very serious affliction to include a much more common condition that people could be more comfortable talking about."

By questioning Pharmacia's assumptions that drugs should be developed only for established medical categories, the team was able to redefine the potential market for Pharmacia's products, turning Detrol into a drug with billion-dollar potential overnight.

Thomas Ebeling brought similar insight to Novartis, challenging some of their existing underlying assumptions. Ebeling remembers:

> "I came over to Novartis from Pepsi, so I was totally new to pharmaceuticals. And that outside perspective freed me to look at the business with fresh eyes. For instance, I realized that my finance people were very focused upon cutting costs. While I acknowledged that cost management and productivity were important, they were not the primary drivers of our profitability.
>
> In a high-risk, high-margin business it is more important to create innovative products which address unmet medical needs and to maximize their sales using clinical product development, life-cycle management, product acquisitions, and strong marketing and sales initiatives."

After all, in markets with this sort of profitability, any increased volume of sales would ultimately net more revenue. When Ebeling became CEO in 2001, he aggressively pursued expansion of Novartis's market presence by purchasing drugs outright, like Pfizer Inc.'s experimental bladder-control drug Enablex. He also entered into development partnerships with large biotech companies like Genentech and bought majority stakes in smaller firms with cutting-edge technology, like U.S. biotech group Idenix Pharmaceuticals. From 2001 to 2002, Novartis's Pharma's total sales grew 13 percent to $13.6 billion. By 2003, sales had increased to $16 billion, an additional increase of 18 percent.

Both of these CEOs were able to improve their company's performance by recognizing and correcting the flawed thinking that hamstrung their respective organizations. It is the quality of their analysis, not their personalities, that was responsible for their corporate performance. In fact, their interpersonal styles had little to do with the fundamental substance that drove their successes.

This observation has been confirmed by empirical data showing that most personality traits have little or no influence on performance ratings.[21] Great leaders have a wide variety of interpersonal styles. Unfortunately, personality and leadership styles still dominate executive evaluations to the exclusion of other, more meaningful, attributes.

All too often conversations about a candidate's qualifications center around personality attributes, such as likability, sense of humor, or polish. While such conversations are often interesting and easily understood, they steal time and focus away from those traits that are the most prominent drivers of performance. Unfortunately, when organizations spend time judging individuals for their style, they typically do so at the expense of evaluating the fundamental aptitudes that actually make a substantial difference in those individuals' success.

# Part Four:
# Style and Personality:
# The Ongoing Distraction

The popularity of emotional intelligence and charismatic leadership, two of the most dominant leadership theories in recent years, has blinded us from seeing what really drives executive success. These concepts are the "herbal supplements" of management science. No one knows for sure if they have any value, but independent research shows them to be nowhere near the level of potency they claim.

And like herbal supplements, leadership theories based on personality or style traits can be dangerous when they supplant more effective treatments. Personality-focused ideas of leadership refer to attributes that at best play a minimal role in performance. When they are included alongside criteria that actually matter, they obscure our ability to identify or develop exceptional talent, and evaluations become clouded with irrelevant and misleading issues.

Let's revisit the primary characteristics that make someone a charismatic leader. Wharton professor Robert House, a prolific and respected researcher in leadership theory, defined the hallmark traits in his landmark work, "A 1976 Theory of Charismatic Leadership." Qualities he listed were: dominating personality, strong conviction in one's own beliefs, a profound desire to influence others, and unusually high self-confidence.[22] Notably absent is any reference to the quality of one's decision-making.

The same deficiency can be seen with emotional intelligence. Leading theorists Daniel Goleman of Rutgers University, Richard Boyatzis of Case Western Reserve University, and Annie McKee of the University of Pennsylvania's Graduate School of Education openly dismiss the differences in the quality of thinking among executives. In their 2003 book, *Primal Leadership*, Goleman and his coauthors state, "We see intellect and clear thinking largely as the characteristics that get someone in the leadership door. Without those fundamental abilities, no entry is allowed . . ."[23]

Underlying this statement is the unfounded assumption that all executives, since they have all gotten in the "leadership door," are equally competent in their "intellect and clear thinking." With this sweeping pronouncement, the authors encourage us to disregard profound differences in cognitive skill levels that actually exist, in favor of the murky and unproductive world of personality and interpersonal style. This is like dismissing the value of penicillin and replacing it with ginseng, without any sound evidence to support such a move.

No personality type or interpersonal style is responsible for excellent performance. But because of the proliferation of high-profile theories based upon these characteristics, the hiring and promotion of individuals continues to be colored by these factors.

Peter Drucker has a harsh view of leadership theories based on style. In the past, he points outs, personality-based leadership was more relevant to success because executives had to serve as cheerleaders and motivators while implementing other people's strategies. But times have changed.

"The CEO needs to provide a clear understanding of when it is time to push here and pull back there," Drucker says, "and when it's time to abandon something. Tomorrow's leader won't be able to lead by charisma. He or she will need to think through the fundamentals so that other people can work productively." [24] Personality and charismatic style are less relevant than ever.

Jim Collins has gone even farther, warning that leaders whose main contribution was a charismatic style were actually negatively correlated with corporate success. In contrast, the best leaders, according to Collins, were quiet, reserved, or even shy. "These leaders are a paradoxical blend of personal humility and professional will. They are more like Lincoln and Socrates than Patton or Caesar." [25]

Still many management theorists continue to stress irrelevant traits such as warmth, empathy, and hopeful outlook as essential to establishing the "resonance" that motivates people toward a common goal. Yet Jim Collins showed "great" company leaders never focused much on inspiration or resonance with their people. Instead, they found that with disciplined thought and disciplined action, motivation issues simply took care of themselves.

Jon Miller of AOL explains further:

> "Unlike the charismatic leader who just asks people to follow them because of who they are, I am asking people to understand what I'm saying. I like it when people adopt what I say as their own because that to me is a sign of success. And if people understand it they will not only sign up for the program but also evangelize it themselves."

In other words, pursuing goals that make sense to other people is the most effective way to inspire workers and maintain their commitment. An executive's charm or enthusiasm in communicating goals is secondary: it is the clarity of thinking behind an initiative which motivates people to enthusiastically pursue a task. Without clear thinking, no easy smile or warm interpersonal demeanor can inspire people's faith for long.

Irene Rosenfeld explains further:

"As a leader, when coming into a new situation, charisma can be useful, because people have a tendency to be influenced by first impressions. So if you're charismatic, it can help you build initial confidence from your team. But in my experience, substance will trump style every time, so charisma without good judgment will not sustain that confidence. The good news is that in the current environment, having weathered all of the debacles from Enron to WorldCom, and Tyco, the value of substance over style has become much clearer."

Jim Kilts sums it up:

"Charisma, warmth, empathy—I think it's great to have all those qualities. None of those things are bad in and of themselves. In fact they are good. But those things without the right answer do you no good.

If you were to ask me, 'What do you wish you were [as a personality type]?' I would say, 'I wish I was charismatic.' But the first thing I would wish for is that I know the right answer—or I know how to get to the right answer. And that's always the trick, that's the key characteristic you need. That doesn't necessarily mean that you are charismatic or have any other particular personality type. It doesn't matter how charismatic you are if you are leading people off a cliff. And we've seen a lot of charismatic and likable leaders do just that."

Though management experts and business leaders alike have cited sharp, disciplined thinking as an essential attribute for star business performance, this is rarely made the focus of executive evaluations. In its place we continue to accept personality and style as a substitute. This pervasive problem throughout the field of executive assessment has been caused by the widespread confusion regarding the difference between characteristics that are directly responsible for performance and those that are only tangentially related.

# CHAPTER 9 SUMMARY

||||||||||||||||||||||||||

- Not one published study has shown emotional intelligence to be a meaningful predictor of job performance beyond what has long been explained by other measures.

- The behaviors that have been widely cited as indicators of emotional intelligence have long been recognized as personality traits.

- Personality type is in no way an indicator of intelligence.

- When it comes to predicting work performance, cognitive-ability tests have been demonstrated to be approximately ten times as powerful as personality assessments.

- The charismatic-leadership movement, whose influence peaked in the late 1990s, was also a theory dominated by personality and style.

- Charismatic leaders often pose a serious threat to the survival of an organization because they frequently try to appear infallible and decisive at the expense of making the right decision.

- Personality is not a differentiator of star talent. It is an individual's facility for clear thinking or intelligence that largely determines their leadership success.

# CHAPTER 10:

# The Cycle of
# Indirect Measures—
# A Revolving Door

The proponents of emotional-intelligence, charismatic-leadership, and personality-based assessment tools are hardly the first or only psychologists to overemphasize attributes that are only loosely related to business performance. In fact, there are a numbing variety of leadership theories and psychologists selling instruments designed to measure them. What becomes confusing is that all of these measures are marketed with impressive statistics which support their correlations to performance. But as any experienced executive will tell you, these assessment methods rarely live up to their promise, and most fade into the background with the emergence of the next leadership fad.

Stephen Kaufman recounts his experience of being constantly bombarded with "the next great theory." During his fourteen-year tenure as CEO of Arrow Electronics, Kaufman increased the company's market capitalization from $40 million to more than $4 billion, making it the world's largest electronics distributor, with over $11 billion in annual sales. Now a senior lecturer at Harvard Business School, Kaufman warns all of his students not to succumb to the never-ending cycle and false promises of management trends.

"In my course I list twenty of the major fad theories that emerged during my career; I can still name each of them and tell you when they came out. But it's always the same. Someone comes along with a little pattern that they've found and starts calling it the 'magic bullet,' and everyone jumps on it. But they all last about eighteen months, until someone else comes along with the next formula to great leadership. Each of these comes with its own three-letter acronym, and after a while it all just becomes alphabet soup—a mind-numbing jumble of letters."

The purveyors of these instruments don't intend to mislead, but they all suffer from the same problem: a fundamental misunderstanding of the differences between a direct versus an indirect measure of performance. And until we understand this distinction, the revolving door of management theories will continue.

This difference can be explained quite simply. Consider some of the more direct indicators of the presence of fire: intense heat and smoke. If you were to attempt to discern the existence of fire solely on the basis of the sound of sirens, you would be mistaken far more often than if you based your conclusion on the presence of intense smoke and heat. That is because an indirect indicator, such as the sound of a siren, could signal many things totally unrelated to fire, such as injury, accident, or a false alarm, whereas intense heat and smoke are nearly always indicators of fire.

The same holds true for management science. Too many psychologists assess performance using measures that are highly indirect and, therefore, dangerously error-prone. Over time, the inaccuracy of these tools is inevitably exposed, but all too often the measurements that come along to replace them suffer from the same fundamental problem: they determine performance based on criteria that are also highly indirect, dooming them to the same fate as their predecessors.

Famed researcher Michael Scriven identified this sloppy practice during the emergence of the teaching styles movement among educators during the 1990s. Research had shown a correlation between a teacher's interpersonal style—for example, the amount of eye contact or frequency of smiles—and the students' rates of learning. As a result teacher training began to emphasize these behaviors. Teachers were encouraged to increase their amount of eye contact or frequency of smiles, and other indicators of warmth.[1]

But something damaging happened as a result. Evaluators who had been informed of the correlation between teaching style and student learning began looking for the presence of these behaviors when they graded teachers' performance. In a sense, the evaluators were listening for sirens, instead of relying on much more direct measures of whether the students were actually learning, such as math or reading proficiency tests. By including indirect criteria, like frequent smiles or head nods, they needlessly diluted the accuracy of their conclusions.

This is like adding too many ingredients to a soup; after a while it becomes impossible to tell whether the base stock is beef, poultry, or vegetable. So if someone asks you what kind of soup it is, their question becomes impossible to answer. The same clouding of truth occurs when highly indirect measures of performance are mixed with more direct measures. It becomes nearly impossible to render an accurate verdict.

Further, including indirect means of evaluating teaching performance also created an unnecessarily high error rate in evaluations. Many effective instructors were unfairly penalized for a "less desirable" teaching style, while other terrible teachers received unwarranted praise.

Regardless of a teacher's style, if students consistently learn at a remarkable rate and report positive attitudes toward learning, no competent evaluator could argue that the teacher is inept. Those two factors—

student learning rates and attitudes—are direct indicators of the quality of the teaching they received. Adding a teacher's propensity to smile to these other criteria is likely to lead to unnecessary evaluative mistakes. And to penalize a teacher for having a reserved personality, even though his or her students learn exceptionally well, violates a basic requirement of evaluation, namely the responsibility to determine the actual merit of an individual's performance.

When judging someone's skills, it is inexcusable to rely upon indirect indicators when more direct measures are readily available. This would be like choosing to determine whether your child has a fever by looking to see if he or she is flushed, as opposed to sticking a thermometer in the child's mouth. A thermometer is a direct measure of the specific question you are trying to answer; a flushed appearance is an indirect sign of many things (a rash, exercise, etc.), of which a fever could be one.

While in the executive arena there is no "thermometer" to provide a direct metric of performance, among the various assessments there is a dramatic range in their level of directness. These variations in large part determine the true evaluative accuracy of these measures, which is so often different from the statistical claims presented in their marketing materials. All of these measures fall on a scale, ranging from the most direct, like a thermometer, to distant characteristics, like a child's irritability. The closer a measure is to the direct end of the scale, the more accurate it is.

Take, for example, a manager's ability to meet deadlines. It is nearly impossible to be a star executive if one consistently comes up short on this requirement. Therefore, meeting deadlines is an essential consideration when evaluating an executive's overall strengths and weaknesses. But how do you measure one's performance in this area?

The most direct method would include keeping a running tabulation of all the deadlines an executive met or missed during the course of his or her career, with each weighted according to its importance. We could then, with precision, calculate the rate at which an executive meets deadlines. But obviously this is not practical in the real world, so we are forced to turn to measures that can be realistically performed.

One such measure, a typical personality test, is often touted as a valid way of assessing someone's propensity for meeting deadlines. This measure might ask questions about an individual's preference for an orderly workspace, or how soon after a task is assigned one prefers to begin work on it. We might say such tests are designed to determine how "anal retentive" an individual is.

While such questions might yield interesting information regarding a person's habits, they are a highly indirect means of answering the key question about meeting deadlines. Plenty of executives keep a very messy desk and still meet deadlines, and many start projects at the last minute and still turn out high-quality work on time. As you see from their place on the scale, personality measures are highly indirect indicators of performance:

## MEASUREMENT ACCURACY

| Personality Tests

| 0% | 25% | 50% | 75% | 100% |
|---|---|---|---|---|
| Least Direct | | | | Most Direct |

A much more direct approach would be a demonstrated-ability test, which would require a candidate to actually break down a variety of different tasks in order to meet a deadline. The individual would be evaluated on his or her ability to differentiate between high-priority and secondary issues, or to identify paths that are likely to bear fruit as opposed to those that will lead to dead-ends. These skills have a direct bearing on one's capacity for meeting deadlines, and are therefore quite predictive of one's ability to do so.

Measures of personality and style are extremely inaccurate when it comes to predicting performance, because they assess behaviors that are only tangentially related to how well an executive actually does his or her job. This explains why independent research has proven them to be very unreliable indicators.[2]

The danger of these measures is that, as with the teaching-style example, they penalize people for oddities of style even when such attributes have no effect on performance. Punishing those who do not fit an idealized "type" perpetuates an unjustified bias and distorts evaluations.

If you were searching for a world-class swimmer, for instance, you could line up the applicants and measure their physical attributes, and you might be able to predict their swimming performance to some extent. But dismissing those who do not meet a preconceived, ideal body-type would be foolish. Talent is rare, hard to find, and does not always come in one specific form. It makes much more sense to put all the candidates in a pool and time them.

None of these criticisms of indirect measures are intended to imply they have *no* intrinsic value. Indirect measures can, in fact, offer interesting descriptive information about an individual. But for business performance, their evaluative accuracy is too tenuous. Any measure—based on personality, working style, or any other theory—that is only indirectly related to how well someone actually does their job, must be barred from a significant role in assessing performance.

Once we recognize that indirect measures will never be very accurate, the revolving door of ineffective leadership fads can be closed. Instead of following fads, we can focus on powerful more direct measures, such as the commonly accepted and widely used Past Behavioral Interview (PBI).

PBIs use questions that ask about an individual's experiences performing certain activities. Most people are very familiar with these job interview questions, such as, "Tell me about a time that you had to juggle multiple, urgent deadlines. How did you handle that?" The candidate is then prompted to choose instances from his or her past and provide details about them.

These interviews offer strong evaluative accuracy because the questions they ask *directly* concern the candidates' ability to perform their job. PBIs are currently the only measures commonly accepted in executive assessment that are highly direct. Their benefits have made them the foremost and virtually the only methodology currently used, so let's explore PBIs more fully.

# CHAPTER 10 SUMMARY

||||||||||||||||||||||||||

- There are a numbing variety of leadership theories and psychologists selling instruments designed to measure them. Yet most of these instruments suffer from the same problem—a fundamental misunderstanding of the differences between a direct versus an indirect measure of performance.

- Direct measures of performance are always dramatically more accurate than indirect measures. As a result, it is inexcusable to rely upon indirect indicators when more direct measures are readily available.

- Measures of personality and style are extremely inaccurate when it comes to predicting performance, because they assess behaviors that are only tangentially related to how well an executive actually does his or her job.

- *Past Behavioral Interviews (PBIs)* are currently the most commonly used executive-assessment measures that are highly direct.

# CHAPTER 11

## Part One:
## The Evolution of
## the Job Interview

|||||||||||||||||||||||||

Early research on the validity of job interviews showed them to be of little value. The first studies suggested one would actually be better off flipping a coin than using an interview to predict someone's work performance.

One of the earliest investigations of interview accuracy was conducted in 1911 by Alfred Binet. In his experiment three experienced teachers interviewed the same five children and estimated their intelligence levels. Each teacher conducted their interviews as they saw fit, and although all three teachers were extremely confident about the accuracy of their results, Binet discovered that their conclusions totally disagreed with one another.[1] As Binet quickly understood, unstructured conversations, even when conducted by experts, were an unreliable means of measuring an individual's intelligence. This insight led him to choose a much more standardized written format for his academic-intelligence test.

Similarly, psychologist Walter Dill Scott, a prolific writer and researcher who later became president of Northwestern University, conducted one of the earliest inquiries into the accuracy of interviews for selecting employees. In 1915, Scott published a study in which he had six personnel managers interview and rank thirty-six prospective employees for a sales job.[2] Interestingly, there was almost no agreement among the personnel managers as to which applicant was most likely to succeed. Even worse, in nearly 77 percent of the cases, managers could not even agree if an applicant should be ranked in the top half or the bottom half of the group. It was an issue of considerable alarm to Scott that personnel managers, the seeming experts in interviewing, could not even concur on whether applicants were above or below average.

Several follow-up studies confirmed Scott's concerns about the accuracy of interviews.[3] One of the most notable of these was conducted by a doctoral student at the University of London named Egbert H. Magson. He was a student of famed psychological researcher and statistician Charles Spearman, who was most widely known for his theory of general intelligence, or "G."

In 1914, at the suggestion of Spearman, Magson began to investigate the value of the "personal interview." As the first scientist to publish a large empirical study on the subject, Magson stressed the importance that potential insights from the study would hold, stating, "In everyday life, one's ability to sell goods, to persuade people to accept a new point of view or doctrine, to get on harmoniously with people in general in all the various occupations of life, depends upon one's ability to estimate the powers, capacities and characteristics of people." Since the personal interview was by far the most commonly used way of making such judgments in occupational settings, Magson felt that a better understanding of its accuracy was essential.[4]

From 1914 through the early 1920s (World War I interrupted for several years), Magson used panels of four to five judges at a time to conduct interviews that would estimate the "intelligence, sense of humor, cheerfulness, quickness, and profoundness" of 149 male students.[5] These categories were chosen because Magson felt these qualities were important for success both in life and on the job. He also administered intelligence tests to each student, and had acquaintances who had been in daily contact with the subjects for at least a year rate each candidate on the traits of interest.

Consistency between the interview estimates and third-party sources (intelligence tests and reference information) averaged about 2 percent. In other words, interview results only negligibly corresponded with the considerably more objective and reliable sources. Magson concluded that these interview ratings could hardly be considered "accurate," calling into question the common practice of using an interview as a valid means of evaluating job candidates.

By 1942, the flow of evidence suggesting the inaccuracy of job interviews led prominent psychologists to call for diminishing the role interviews had in assessing candidates. E. F. Wonderlic, one of the most prominent psychologists in this field at the time, summarized the general concern. "As a procedure, interviewing is not useful for obtaining facts; all important information obtained in an interview should be verified by one means or another—by checking references, by credit investigation, by inspection, etc. Interviewing is not a good device for measuring mental ability or job skills, nor is it particularly useful in discovering hidden aptitudes of possible candidates."[6]

As the diagram shows, these early interviewing practices had almost no ability to illuminate much about an individual's performance. However, these early quantitative results did set researchers on the path to finding an interview methodology that would work.

ACCURACY OF EARLY INTERVIEW PRACTICES

Interview Accuracy

100%

75%

50%

25%

0%

Early Interview Practices (2–3%)

# Part Two: A Step in the Right Direction

||||||||||||||||||||||||

In 1945, University of California–Berkeley psychology professor Edwin Ghiselli began working with a financial services firm to help it improve hiring practices.[7] He tried to identify the activities that account executives had to perform well in order to succeed. These included strong interpersonal skills, dedicated and responsive work ethic, and sound judgment about financial decisions. Over the next twenty years, he interviewed 507 potential new hires, following a highly structured chronological format. First he asked them about their education, and then he inquired about their previous job experiences. For each of these topics, he asked questions that enumerated their responsibilities and described their performance. There were no questions of a "personal" nature. Instead, the interviews focused only on past experiences that directly related to the activities candidates would have to perform as an account executive.

Ghiselli graded each applicant's potential on a 5-point scale. He then correlated his interview grade with success at the firm after three years of employment. When candidate interview grades were compared with their occupational success, the results were significant. Ghiselli's interviewing method was predicting performance with substantial accuracy.

This work was the genesis of the Past Behavioral Interview (PBI). In 1966, Ghiselli published an article about his new interviewing methodology[8], and his work was subsequently adopted by many other researchers and practitioners in management science.

By the 1980s, subsequent research had proven PBIs to be a valid assessment tool, explaining approximately 25–30 percent of the variance in performance ratings.[9] These figures highlighted a remarkable achievement: PBIs offered more than ten times the accuracy of early job interviews. The long debate regarding whether or not an interview could actually be used to accurately predict performance had finally come to a close.

In 1989, Cornell University psychologist Robert Eder, Texas A&M University's Michele Kacmar, and Gerald Ferris of University of Illinois at Urbana-Champaign, published a summary of the job interview research to that date, including the more recent findings regarding the validity of PBIs, and commented, "Perhaps the century long quest for a more reliable standardized interview form was reaching fruition."[10]

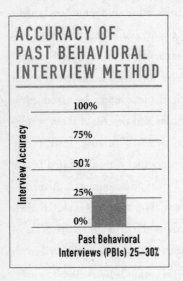

ACCURACY OF
PAST BEHAVIORAL
INTERVIEW METHOD

Interview Accuracy

100%

75%

50%

25%

0%

Past Behavioral
Interviews (PBIs) 25–30%

By the 1990s, Past Behavioral Interviews had come to dominate executive assessment, which was not surprising, considering the vast improvement that these interviews represented over early practices. Today, PBIs have become the standard for any executive assessment across industries. But as good as this methodology is compared to those from the past, it is not the "magic bullet" that it is often purported to be.

# Part Three:
# The Limits of
# Past Behavioral
# Interviews (PBIs)

||||||||||||||||||||||||||

For the past twenty years PBIs have been widely accepted as the best practice in executive evaluation. Today, every major executive search and
assessment firm uses them to measure *all* of a candidate's key strengths
and weaknesses. But using PBIs as an all-purpose tool is overreaching.
Like any individual measure, PBIs are by no means complete; there is a
limit to how much the methodology can tell you about an individual.

Independent research has proven PBIs to be a powerful predictor of
performance. But this same research has shown that the interviews do
not explain the majority of the differences in performance between individuals.[11] A perfect measure would be one that explains 100 percent of
the variance between people, but no such tool exists. Human beings are
simply too complex for any individual measure to explain everything that
makes one person different from another.

Research regarding PBIs shows them to measure about 25 percent of
the variance between individuals.[12] While this number may seem small to
those unfamiliar with statistical analysis, it is actually quite impressive. It
demonstrates that a single conversation can be used to explain approxi-

mately one-quarter of what makes someone more successful than someone else (in terms of work performance).

But these numbers leave significant room for improvement. So in order to understand how PBIs can be improved or supplemented, it is necessary to examine what they actually measure and, more important, what they leave unmeasured. By doing so, we will be able to discern what keeps them from being more complete.

# CHAPTER 11 SUMMARY

||||||||||||||||||||||||||

- Early research on the validity of job interviews showed them to be of little value when it came to predicting work performance.

- PBIs were the first reliable job-interview format, and today are routinely included in nearly every executive evaluation.

- Though PBIs have become widely accepted as the best practice in executive evaluation, there is a limit to how much the methodology can tell you about an individual (approximately 25–30 percent of variance in performance).

- While they represent a significant advance from early interview techniques, PBIs are not the magic bullet that they have been purported to be.

# CHAPTER 12

## Part One:
## The Mystery of Past
## Behavioral Interviews

|||||||||||||||||||||||||

After eighty years of searching, management scientists had finally discovered an interviewing methodology that could accurately predict executive performance, and practitioners began to adopt it in large numbers. In the world of executive assessment today, PBIs are widely touted as the Holy Grail—a single, all-encompassing process that can provide a clear picture of each and every one of an individual's strengths and weaknesses and predict his or her leadership capability.

Although PBIs have been nearly universally adopted in executive assessment practice, there is a fundamental misunderstanding of what these interviews actually measure. While PBIs do predict performance, what gives them accuracy has until now been poorly understood.

This is akin to the early discovery of lime juice as an effective means of preventing scurvy. The disease had been one of the primary causes of death among sailors for centuries. In 1740, British admiral George A. Anson and his Scottish naval surgeon, James Lind, set sail to circumnavigate the globe with a fleet of six ships and 1,955 men. By the end of their voyage, 1,051 had died, almost all from scurvy. Following this tragedy, Dr.

Lind worked to find a cure, and in 1747 he discovered that lime juice was an effective way to stave off the disease. By 1795 the British admiralty had required the distribution of daily doses of lime juice for all sailors.[1]

Although lime juice was indeed an effective antidote for scurvy, the reason why was not understood until 1932, when ascorbic acid (vitamin C) was found to be the reason limes worked so well.[2] Once scientists realized what made the treatment so effective, they went on to synthesize the vitamin in its pure form, and, as a result, scurvy was finally relegated to an easily treated, preventable malady.

PBIs pose a similar mystery. While there is little doubt that the interviews effectively predict performance, the reason why has been poorly understood. This has resulted in a huge measurement gap and has, to a large extent, created the critical shortage of Executive Intelligence at the top of most organizations. Until PBIs are recognized for what they can and cannot measure, we will never understand their limitations, nor will we be able to overcome them. More important, as long as we believe that PBIs offer comprehensive assessment, the essential role of Executive Intelligence will never be fully realized.

The management sciences, like any other field of scientific inquiry, are constantly evolving. What we know to be "true" today is very different from what we knew fifty years ago, and very different from what we'll discover fifty years from now. Stanford biochemistry professor and Nobel laureate Paul Berg has pointed out, "Science progresses oftentimes in fits and starts. There will be things that come up that had not been anticipated. But it's also surprises that energize the science."[3]

There is a surprise when it comes to PBIs: they do not measure what they purport to.

This statement may appear almost blasphemous to an industry totally dependent on this methodology, but it's true. This fundamental underlying problem with PBIs has never before been identified, and it is the main reason there is often a disconnect between a candidate's performance on the PBI assessment and his or her on-the-job performance. This is also why PBIs explain 25–30 percent of the variance between individuals, rather than 65–70 percent.

Through the use of interview questions, PBI assessments are supposed to measure performance on specific activities, called "competencies." These competencies typically include categories like Strategy Development, Resolving Conflict, and Sensitivity to Others. Human resource managers have assumed that by asking questions about all of the competencies germane to a particular position, they would fully understand an executive's relevant skills. And those marketing PBIs have assured them this was the case. Evaluators have viewed the PBI as all-encompassing because they felt sure they were getting a comprehensive idea of a candidate's strengths and weaknesses.

If this were true—if PBIs measured all the components necessary for work success—you would expect PBIs to be the most powerful predictor of job performance. IQ tests, for instance, were designed to measure only one aspect of performance: intelligence. Yet, surprisingly, no published validity study has ever found PBIs to be more accurate at predicting performance than common IQ tests.

The most comprehensive study of this issue was conducted in 1992 by Professor Stephan Motowidlo of the University of Florida and several of his colleagues. In three studies of the PBI involving more than five hundred candidates in corporate management and marketing positions, they found the average correlation between PBI scores and performance ratings to be .22.[4]

Compare this to the 2003 study by Professor Jesus Salgado of the University of Santiago and his colleagues, involving 783 managers.[5] The correlation between IQ test scores and job performance was .25. These findings are by no means anomalies. They are consistent with numerous other independent examinations of these assessment methodologies.[6]

These results raise the question: Why, if PBIs are measuring all the essential skills for a specific job, are their correlations to job performance no higher than that of an IQ test?

The answer, once again, is that PBIs do not measure what they claim to. Take, for example, two sample PBI questions. The first, *"What is the strategic direction of your company/division and how did you go about developing it?"* is designed to assess someone's performance on strategy development. The second, *"Describe a situation where you had to interact with a difficult colleague and diffuse your interpersonal differences,"* is supposed to test a person's capacity to resolve conflict.

What is surprising is that one can just as accurately predict an executive's strategy-development performance from his or her answer to the *resolving conflict* question, as by using his or her score on the *strategic-development question*. And this is not just a single example unique to these two competency questions. The same circumstance holds true for *any* competency question: one is equally predictive of any other. Every published study on this subject has yielded the same conclusion.*

The following figure compares the *expected* results from competency interview questions to their *actual* results:

---

*This problem was commented on by Professor Motowidlo and his colleagues in their widely cited 1992 study regarding the validity of the PBI. In examining the correlations between 17 different competencies rated first in the interview and then by the candidate's supervisors, they found no evidence that their interview questions were actually measuring the competencies they were intended to assess. In 1999, Professors James Conway and Gina Peneno of Seton Hall University further examined this phenomenon using PBI interviews with 175 job applicants. They too concluded that there was no evidence that the questions were actually tapping the intended competencies. These findings were once again replicated in 2001 by Bradley University professor Allen Huffcutt and his colleagues, in their article summarizing the results of 47 different empirical studies on the subject.

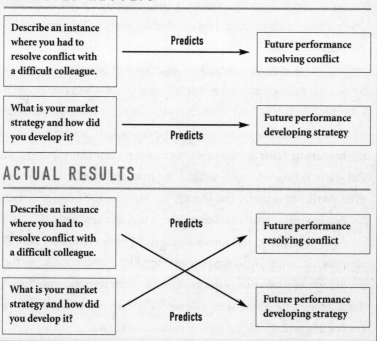

This confounding outcome can be best understood by taking an analogy from sports. If you want to accurately determine how fast someone can swim a lap, you can time him or her in the pool from start to finish. Further, if you want to find out how high someone can jump, you can have the person jump and measure the height he or she achieves. But no one would reasonably argue that you can just as accurately predict someone's swim lap time by measuring how high he or she jumps, or vice versa. Yet this is exactly what happens with PBIs.

With PBIs you are just as accurate in determining a candidate's proficiency on one competency by looking at his or her interview score on any other competency. Clearly, there must be an underlying driver or drivers common to all the competencies, which are the true subjects of a PBI measurement.

So for instance, in the swimming and jumping example, a common driver might be leg strength. This could affect your speed in the pool and the height that you reach in a jump. In a manner of speaking, PBIs are measuring leg strength—an underlying driver that cuts across all competencies. We must identify what that is—what is really being measured by PBIs. Because just as there are factors other than leg strength that determine one's speed in swimming laps (arm strength, stamina, etc.), so might there be other drivers of job success that are totally missed by the PBI. Here is how we finally unravel the mystery behind the ceiling on PBIs' predictive accuracy and identify the other methodologies that can be used to yield a much more complete picture of a candidate.

What does this mean? Are we saying that PBI interviews are not reliable when it comes to assessing performance? Of course not. Clearly they are capable of predicting performance to some degree. But until we understand what the limits of the PBI are, we will never understand how to reach a dramatically higher level of assessment accuracy.

# Part Two: What Do PBIs Actually Measure?

||||||||||||||||||||||||||||

What is the answer to the PBI mystery? In 2002, Professors Jesus Salgado and Silvia Moscoso of the University of Santiago conducted a massive analysis of PBIs and finally revealed why the results of every PBI question, regardless of the topic, appeared indistinguishable. By combining the results of hundreds of independent empirical studies on the subject, they found that an individual's performance on any PBI question was dominated by the same three things: experience, job knowledge, and social skills.[7]

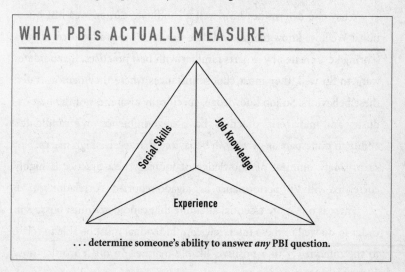

**WHAT PBIs ACTUALLY MEASURE**

Social Skills

Job Knowledge

Experience

. . . determine someone's ability to answer *any* PBI question.

Just as leg strength is a broad determinant of an individual's performance across many different sporting activities—experience, job knowledge, and social skills are all broad drivers that determine an executive's performance on *any* competency. Let's examine the reasons why each of these drivers plays such a prominent role in a candidate's ability to score well in these interviews.

During a typical PBI interview, candidates are asked questions that require them to recount their experiences with the competencies identified as necessary for the job. For instance, they may be asked a series of questions about their history of managing resources. Any candidate tends to portray himself or herself in a flattering light, by focusing on positive examples from their past. Those who have a longer work history generally have more experiences to draw upon, allowing them to select and detail a couple of especially impressive and self-flattering stories. For this reason experience has a huge influence on one's ability to do well on PBIs. In fact, Salgado found the "number of years worked" has an overwhelming effect on a candidate's PBI scores (correlation = .71).

What else determines how well a candidate can answer PBI questions? Well, we know that a candidate's answers are graded according to scoring keys created by experts familiar with best practices. If candidates want to do well, they must choose instances where they demonstrated these behaviors. So job knowledge, specifically awareness of the best industry and managerial practices, has a huge influence on a candidate's ability to punctuate answers with behaviors that receive high marks. Not surprisingly, amount of knowledge of industry best-practice is highly correlated with PBI performance, as Salgado reported (correlation = .53).

There is one more essential attribute that candidates must possess in order to do well in these interviews. An individual must be able to relate to the interviewer in a positive, likable manner. In other words, those with strong social skills have a distinct advantage during these in-person evaluations. Similarly, social skills also play a very large role in PBI performance (correlation = .65).

Experience, job knowledge, and social skills—these are what determine how well a person answers any PBI question, regardless of the topic or competency. There's no doubt that these three drivers are important for any executive to have, and what makes the PBI so predictive is that it repeatedly assesses these essential attributes. Even so, these three factors take us only so far when it comes to identifying star talent.

As Jon Miller, AOL's CEO, explains:

> "As someone who interviews a lot of potential employees in various capacities, I have a theory that if you've survived in business to a certain point, and done reasonably well, you probably present yourself well, have a good base of business knowledge, and you have a good story. Yet none of those things are enough to tell you whether someone is actually going to excel in your organization or not. They've had a chance to hone their story; we all learn to do that over time. But how well someone tells their story is not enough."

Miller understands the limitations of the information offered by PBIs. While he concedes that they certainly are of value, particularly in establishing a candidate's minimum qualifications, he also points out that they offer only an incomplete understanding of an individual's capabilities.

Take experience, for example, which dominates performance in the PBI interview. Obviously experience is important: having done something before undoubtedly helps you when you try to do it again. But experience is not the only mark of a great leader. Star leaders do the right thing far more often than they stumble, in other words their ratio of success to failure is unusually high, especially compared to that of their peers. While experience often helps, we all know "seasoned" executives who aren't stars. So obviously experience alone is not enough.

Job knowledge raises similar issues. While it is a useful attribute for any manager, knowledge alone does not make someone excel. Just as two surgeons may both have equal training and be familiar with the best way to carry out a particular procedure, one doctor may consistently achieve better results. Some surgeons are simply more skillful, even if their knowledge is the same as their colleagues'. Knowledge of best practices is not enough; it is the skill with which executives apply their knowledge that determines whether or not they outperform their peers.

Finally, social skills unquestionably have a strong influence on someone's appeal; they are important for any manager to have. But, they have no bearing on the quality of an individual's decisions. How many highly likable individuals do you know who do not possess the intellectual horsepower to be a star leader? Social skills, while relevant, do not make someone a great executive.

Bob Davies, the CEO of Church & Dwight, explains further:

> "The traditional interview process is a kind of show-and-tell. Candidates are expected to highlight their most positive experiences in order to get the job. This creates an artificial situation. But no matter how diligent you are about your interview and reference-checking practices, it's roughly fifty-fifty whether you will end up with a good hire—and those are terrible odds."

As Davies points out, no matter how well you conduct your interview, there are limitations to the power it has to predict a candidate's success. So what does this mean for the field of executive assessment? PBIs remain an excellent way to test three of the essential drivers of performance: experience, job knowledge, and social skills. But now that we know what the interviews actually measure, there's no need to explore each and every competency with exhaustive questioning, since each question is essentially assessing the same three things. We need only ask enough questions to get a reliable appraisal of a candidate's experience, job knowledge, and social skills. Beyond that, the PBI is unlikely to add anything to the overall accuracy of the evaluation.

Because hiring managers have been told that PBIs can be used to assess any skill relevant to a particular job position, they have turned these interviews into grueling exercises. Today it has become common for executives to endure marathon PBI assessments that go on for three to four hours. Candidates are required to provide countless, highly detailed descriptions of their professional experiences that showcase their use of best managerial practices in every competency thought to have value. Although these interviews generate large volumes of detailed anecdotes about an individual, the considerable amount of time they require does not improve the overall accuracy of the assessment. In fact, more time will never make PBIs more complete. There is simply only so much information that they can reveal.

As useful as they nonetheless are, PBIs possess a startling flaw. They totally fail to measure one core attribute that is absolutely vital to executive performance: intelligence.

Several studies have established this beyond a doubt. The most definitive research was a large-scale work published in 1996 by Professors Allen Huffcutt of Bradley University, Philip Roth of Clemson University, and Michael McDaniel of the University of Akron. Calculating the statistical average from forty-nine independent empirical studies, they found the overlap between PBIs and intelligence tests to be just 3 percent.[8]

This matches the findings of the other large-scale study on the subject, conducted in 2002 by Professors Jesus Salgado and Silvia Moscoso.[9] Combining the findings from twenty-two independent empirical studies in the European Union, involving over three thousand candidates, they found the overlap between intelligence tests and the PBI to be only 4 percent, almost identical to the number found in 1996 by Huffcutt and his colleagues.

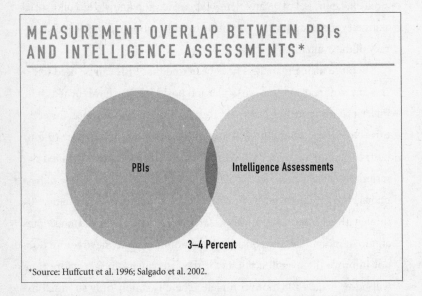

## MEASUREMENT OVERLAP BETWEEN PBIs AND INTELLIGENCE ASSESSMENTS*

PBIs

Intelligence Assessments

3–4 Percent

*Source: Huffcutt et al. 1996; Salgado et al. 2002.

This is a very serious problem. Cognitive ability, or intelligence, has been proven to be one of the most powerful predictors of managerial success. Yet the most widely used executive-assessment methodology, the PBI, totally fails to measure it. How did this startling oversight occur? Because PBIs were thought to measure **every** skill or competency relevant to a particular job, naturally it was taken for granted that they would also account for a candidate's intelligence along the way. It is now clear that this assumption was not valid.

The easiest solution to this problem would be to find a way to adapt PBI questions to measure intelligence. But as we will soon learn, PBI questions are fundamentally incapable of doing so. Why? Because, what is common to all three drivers measured by the PBI is that they are essentially knowledge-based; knowledge that is gained from experience, training in best practices, or social interactions. But intelligence is a very different animal. And until we make clear the difference between knowledge and intelligence, the essential role of cognitive abilities in leadership performance will never be realized.

# CHAPTER 12 SUMMARY

||||||||||||||||||||||||||

- Past Behavioral Interviews (PBIs) have been touted as a single, all-encompassing means to provide a clear picture of each and every one of an individual's strengths and weaknesses and to predict his or her leadership capability.

- Although PBIs have been nearly universally adopted in executive-assessment practice, there is a fundamental misunderstanding of what these interviews actually measure.

- Surprisingly, PBIs do not measure what they claim.

- Research has proven that an individual's performance on any PBI question, regardless of the topic, is dominated by the same three drivers: *experience, job knowledge,* and *social skills.*

- Most important, PBIs totally fail to measure an attribute that is an *essential* determinant of executive performance—intelligence.

# CHAPTER 13

# The Difference Between Knowledge and Intelligence

A comprehensive evaluation of an executive must go beyond simply testing his or her knowledge. We must understand how to include an appropriate measure of intelligence, or there will always be a huge gap in the evaluation of any candidate. The question is how do we build such a test? The first step toward this goal is to understand the difference between knowledge and intelligence.

According to Joseph Fagan, the chair of Case Western Reserve University's psychology department, the confusion between the two concepts is an important ongoing problem in the field: "My belief is that controversy surrounding the term intelligence has arisen and continues because intelligence has historically been defined as how much one knows rather than how well one processes."[1] Fagan's research focused on racial differences in test scores, and his experiments found that measures that required certain kinds of academic knowledge, such as vocabulary or complex math, yielded significantly different scores between racial groups. But tests focused on reasoning or processing skills, such as picture and spatial pattern recognition, showed no such differences.

Unfortunately, the distinction between knowledge and intelligence is frequently blurred. For example, most people are familiar with the popular television show *Jeopardy!*, on which contestants are rewarded for the amount of knowledge they possess of a wide variety of topics. Often the winners are referred to as "exceptionally smart." But the truth is that they are exceptionally knowledgeable. Successful *Jeopardy!* contestants haven't really proven anything about their intelligence. They have only demonstrated an unusual—and impressive—facility for the recitation of facts. And while recalling the facts about a particular topic can be useful, it has little to do with intelligence, which refers to how skillfully one uses a given set of facts to achieve a particular goal. For instance, an individual who accurately identifies the hidden assumptions in a colleague's argument is demonstrating intelligence, whereas someone who overhears a discussion of these assumptions and later repeats that explanation in a subsequent debate is not. The latter is merely showing off knowledge gained from witnessing an intelligent analysis.

Stephen Carter, CEO of Superior Essex, expands further:

"There are many people who know a lot about their industry and are very experienced. So they assume that what they have to say must be relevant. They want to participate in meetings and feel they ought to say something, so they just restate what someone else said, or just blindly attack other people's ideas. The problem is that they are not thinking; they are just talking."

As Carter notes, knowledge applied without intelligence is of little use. Few people have articulated the importance of intelligence better than Jack Welch:

"I've always weighted the quality of an individual over their industry knowledge. Take for example Bob Wright, now chairman and CEO of NBC/Universal. Bob started out as a lawyer. He then worked with me in plastics, housewares, and finally GE Capital, before I made him president of NBC in 1986. People wondered how a guy from GE could run a major television network. But it's always been my belief that industry knowledge can be gained by someone with good thinking skills. If they bring that to the party, they can assess the new environment and get a feel for the business very quickly."

What Welch values is a person's ability to analyze and process information—their intelligence. And it is hard to underestimate the power of these cognitive skills when it comes to business success. Welch is not saying that knowledge is irrelevant, but rather that knowledge and intelligence are interdependent.

If we compare knowledge and intelligence to the functions of a computer, we can see that knowledge is like data that can be stored on a hard drive, to be called upon when needed. Simply knowing what is contained on a hard drive, however, tells us nothing about how efficiently that information will be used.

No matter how much we examine what information is on the hard drive, we cannot get any insight about the computer's processor . . . and the processor is central to the functioning of the machine. One computer may not have enough processing power to effectively analyze the data already on its hard drive; another computer may be able to rapidly process that data plus a great deal more, with exceptional effectiveness.

Knowledge-based measures can only tell us what is contained on an individual's hard drive. To be able to fully predict an individual's performance, we need to know his or her processing power—*intelligence*.

Knowledge provides essential clues to the best way to handle a particular situation, yet this information is useful only to the degree that it is skillfully applied. Intelligence is the information processor that determines how deftly one's knowledge will be used.

Both knowledge and intelligence are necessary for a good solution. Just as knowledge is not useful if it cannot be intelligently applied, intelligence is useless without sufficient knowledge to process. Unfortunately, present executive assessments focus purely on knowledge, providing no measure of intelligence.

Kevin Rollins, CEO of Dell, recognizes the irreplaceable value of processing power and its relationship to success. But, as he points out, intelligence is hard to find. It is so rare, in fact, that the vast majority of Dell's senior executives come from outside the computer industry. Rollins explains:

> "We commit a tremendous amount of energy to finding highly skilled people to hire. We value the quality of a person over their industry experience. If people have the right skills, they can learn what they need to know about our industry. More importantly, they will ask questions and probe into what we do with a fresh set of eyes. We can teach our leaders and team members the tenets of our model, but we can't teach them to be smart."

As Rollins points out, knowledge can never be considered a replacement for intelligence. Yet current assessment practices focus almost exclusively on knowledge. So how do we ensure that we can adequately assess a candidate's processing power? The key is to create a tool that measures intelligence, one that can be combined with existing assessments of knowledge, such as the PBI. This will yield a radically more complete evaluation of a candidate.

In fact, because there is al-most no overlap between measures of intelligence and knowledge (just 3–4 percent), adding an intelligence compo-nent to current assessment practices yields a dramatic improvement—nearly dou-bling the accuracy.

So our work begins with recognizing that intelligence questions for executives must focus on how well a manager uses or ma-nipulates information or knowledge. Of course, creating measures of an individual's processing power is no easy feat. While no current measure is appropriate for the executive population, it is not as if no measures of in-telligence exist. So that is where we can start. By using existing intelligence questions—and seeing how they differ from knowledge questions—we can create an assessment that is tailored to Executive Intelligence.

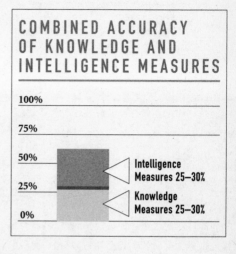

COMBINED ACCURACY OF KNOWLEDGE AND INTELLIGENCE MEASURES

100%
75%
50%
25%
0%

Intelligence Measures 25–30%
Knowledge Measures 25–30%

# CHAPTER 13 SUMMARY

|||||||||||||||||||||||||||

- In order to create an appropriate test of Executive Intelligence we must first understand the difference between knowledge and intelligence.

- Knowledge refers to information that one can recall about a subject, while intelligence determines how skillfully one uses such information to achieve a particular goal.

- Knowledge and intelligence are interdependent. One cannot be applied effectively without the other, and they are both necessary to reach a sound conclusion.

- The most common executive-assessment methodologies focus purely on knowledge and provide no measure of intelligence.

- Adding an intelligence measure to currently existing knowledge assessments would nearly double the predictive accuracy of evaluations.

# CHAPTER 14

## Part One:
## How Does One
## Measure Intelligence?

|||||||||||||||||||||||||||

Knowledge and intelligence are distinct concepts and, therefore, each requires its own kind of measure. Knowledge questions require someone to recite what he or she has learned or experienced, while intelligence questions call for an individual to perform a task. By definition, knowledge questions require no problem solving or processing of new information, so they are fundamentally incapable of yielding direct measures of a candidate's intelligence. These distinctions can be more clearly understood by comparing the two types of questions—those that measure knowledge and those that measure intelligence.

An evaluator might ask a candidate the following knowledge question about managing costs:

> *Let's talk about ways that you've succeeded in maximizing profits for your shareholders. What specifically have you done to reduce costs in your company?*

Candidates typically respond by recounting experiences that show how they have managed costs in the past, ideally with measurable, positive results. A strong response to this question might be:

"I have a consistent, proven track record of implementing successful cost-containment strategies. For instance, in my first year as CEO, I shifted all equipment purchases to an online bidding system with suppliers, vastly increasing competition among them and saving an average of 10 percent on all purchases. I also created an internal travel agency with responsibility for managing all travel costs. That saved us 25 million in our first year alone . . ."

Here, the candidate has included detailed examples of her knowledge regarding current managerial best practices. This individual has also given specifics about experiences implementing these techniques. The more such instances candidates can provide, the more knowledge they can be assumed to have regarding this topic and, accordingly, the better they do on the evaluation.

Here's another knowledge question, one that concerns teamwork:

*Now let's talk about your track record promoting teamwork. Can you tell me some specific instances in which you've had to sacrifice your own wishes for the good of the team?*

An impressive candidate might answer as follows:

"Absolutely. There is nothing I stress more than the importance of teamwork. I changed our executive performance evaluations to make that one of our central criteria. Everyone is evaluated on how well they have shared their best ideas with others, coached their coworkers, and pursued the best interests of the group over their own. Also, during our last round of budget cuts, we had to freeze all wage increases throughout the company. But to remind our people that we all sacrifice as a team, I took a 50 percent pay cut until the wage freezes ended."

This candidate recites instances of his use of best-practice team-building activities. These types of questions are very appropriate because they require a candidate to respond "on their feet" with clarity, which is similar to how executives have to work. The question topics directly assess a candidate's knowledge regarding important work activities. Such inquiries are easily tolerated by executives because they are conversational, and they seem fair and highly relevant. But neither of these questions offer any way to assess the candidate's facility for *processing* information.

Now we begin to understand why research has consistently shown so little overlap between someone's ability to answer knowledge questions and his or her facility for scoring well on intelligence tests. It is because you cannot measure an individual's intelligence by asking how smart he or she is, or has been in the past. These types of "self-report" questions allow candidates to select experiences that show desirable behaviors, making it an exercise in knowledge retrieval. In other words, their ability to recall and recite examples that show managerial best practices dominates their interview score. Intelligence plays almost no role in the measure. Using the computer analogy, these questions look only at what files and data are contained on the hard drive; they do nothing to test an individual's processing power.

What distinguishes an intelligence question from a knowledge question? Simply put, an intelligence question asks the candidate to solve a new problem, whereas a knowledge question merely asks a candidate to recall information.

Yale professor Robert Sternberg, president of the American Psychological Association and a leading expert in intelligence measurement, helped to clarify these distinctions when he pointed out that only certain types of questions measure intelligence. He explained, "No one would believe that all problem-solving tasks are equally apt as measures of intelligence: Solving the problem of what to eat for lunch on a typical day scarcely seems to be in the same class as, say, solving the problem of identifying hidden assumptions in a colleague's argument as a measure of intelligence. Even within a given problem type, some problems seem to provide more apt measures of intelligence than do others. A verbal analogy that could be solved solely on the basis of knowing the meanings of the words in the analogy would seem to be a less apt measure of intelligence than a verbal analogy that required not only some vocabulary but also complex reasoning."[1] Intelligence questions must, he concluded, involve problem solving that cannot be demonstrated through the recitation of previously acquired knowledge.

Therefore, he suggests, measures of intelligence must utilize questions and situations that a candidate has never confronted before. Only by having someone actually solve a problem can you be sure that you are measuring the candidate's intelligence, rather than his or her capacity to repeat a solution previously witnessed, heard of, or read about. The more novel the situation, the less rote knowledge can be applied, and the more cognitive ability is required for the answer.

Now let's take a look at a few typical IQ test questions that are designed to measure intelligence.[2]

**1. Which number should come next in this series?**

3, 5, 8, 13, 21,

(a) 23                          (c) 24

(b) 34                          (d) 41

The correct answer to this question is 34. As you can see, to figure out the number that comes next you must add the two previous numbers in the sequence. These questions are designed to test pattern recognition, logic, and mathematical intelligence.

2. *Library* is to *book* as *book* is to:

(a) page                        (c) binding

(b) copy                        (d) cover

The correct answer to this question is *page*. Books are found within libraries, just as pages are found within books. This type of question is designed to measure logical reasoning and verbal intelligence.

3. Pick the piece that's missing from the diagram on the left.

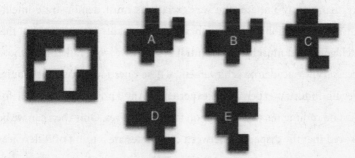

The correct answer to this question is C. By rotating each of the figures so that they are oriented the same as the puzzle, it becomes apparent that C is the only one that fits. This question is designed to test spatial reasoning aptitude.

All three of these questions require a candidate to use the information provided in order to deduce the answer. No previous knowledge, other than the most rudimentary common to any adult, is required. While these questions do indeed measure an individual's processing power, they are not appropriate for executives for several reasons.

First, they appear in a written multiple-choice format and have only one right answer. No executive problem ever presents itself in this manner. Real-life problems have multiple possible solutions and are almost always addressed through verbal encounters. Second, the cognitive skills assessed, including spatial reasoning, arithmetic, and verbal analogies, are not central to executive success. Executive responsibilities rarely involve these aptitudes. Finally, the topics appear so academic and elementary that they are viewed as insulting by those with extensive professional experience.

In order to create an appropriate intelligence measure for executives, we need to combine the verbal interview format of traditional knowledge questions with the processing power demands of IQ tests. This will yield a tool that not only measures intelligence, but does so using a methodology that closely imitates the way executives must demonstrate intelligence on the job. Further, the cognitive skills measured by this intelligence test must be those central to executive work rather than those necessary for academic achievement. These questions must not require specific industry expertise or experience. Any knowledge they call for must be rudimentary and common to all executives. Only then can we be assured that the disparities between candidates are a result of differences in their processing power, not their knowledge.

So what are the specific cognitive skills that need to be measured by these questions? They are the cognitive skills associated with Executive Intelligence.

# INDIVIDUAL SKILLS THAT COMPRISE EXECUTIVE INTELLIGENCE

| Regarding Tasks, Great Leaders:[3] | Regarding People, Great Leaders:[4] | Regarding Oneself, Great Leaders:[5] |
|---|---|---|
| Appropriately define a problem and differentiate essential objectives from less relevant concerns. | Recognize the conclusions that can and cannot be drawn from a particular exchange. | Pursue and encourage feedback that may reveal an error in judgment and then make appropriate adjustments. |
| Anticipate likely obstacles to achieving objectives and identify sensible means to circumvent them. | Recognize the likely underlying agendas and motivations of individuals and groups that are involved in a situation. | Demonstrate an ability to recognize one's own personal biases or limitations in perspective, and use this understanding to improve one's own thinking and plans for action. |
| Critically examine the accuracy of the underlying assumptions being relied on. | Anticipate the likely emotional reactions of individuals to actions or communications. | Recognize when serious flaws in one's own ideas or actions require swift public acknowledgment of the mistake and a dramatic change in direction. |
| Articulate the strengths and weaknesses of the suggestions or arguments posed by others. | Accurately identify the core issues and perspectives that are central to a conflict. | Appropriately articulate the essential flaws in the arguments of others, and reiterate the strengths of one's own position. |
| Recognize what is known about an issue, what more needs to be known, and how best to obtain the relevant and accurate information needed. | Appropriately consider the probable effects and likely unintended consequences that may result from taking a particular course of action. | Recognize when it is appropriate to resist the objections of others and remain committed to a sound course of action. |
| Use multiple perspectives to identify likely unintended consequences of various action-plans. | Recognize and balance the different needs of all relevant stakeholders. | |

When viewing the skills listed, it is clear that they are all activities that are dependent on how well one processes the information available in order to render a sound conclusion. But we cannot simply ask candidates if they possess these skills. We must have them demonstrate such skills. For instance, rather than asking someone to recount an occasion when they successfully recognized relevant *unintended consequences* of a strategy, a factual situation can be presented that would contain important unintended consequences. The candidates would then be required to demonstrate their facility for this skill.

Until now, it has been believed that such ability tests could not be reliably administered using an interview format. Management scientists favor multiple-choice tests for evaluating intelligence because of such tests' perceived objectivity. It is assumed that human judges in any evaluation, including an interview, inevitably create inaccuracy. If we are to build an appropriate measure of Executive Intelligence, we must first dispel this mistaken assumption.

# Part Two: Test Format— A Crucial Ingredient

|||||||||||||||||||||||||

In 1926, the Scholastic Aptitude Test (SAT) was introduced by the Educational Testing Service (ETS) to assess the academic abilities of high school students. The test's multiple-choice-question formats have remained consistent for eighty years, until 2005, when the SAT was revised to include essay-writing exercises. This represented a profound change in the test. It meant that SAT scores would now be in large part generated by human judges, who would be required to read and grade the overall quality of each student's essay.

Why would ETS institute such a radical change in a test that had become universally accepted? And, wouldn't the introduction of human judges reduce the overall accuracy of the results? Essays graded by humans would seem rife with subjectivity and offer none of the apparent accuracy of computer-scored multiple-choice questions. In terms of conventional wisdom, it would appear that ETS had inexplicably taken a step backward regarding the precision of its most important and widely used test.

Actually, contrary to public perception, ETS's changes were designed to greatly improve the predictive accuracy of SAT results. It was a move based both on sound logic and extensive empirical support. In the years leading up to the revision, an increasing number of major universities had found that essay-based standardized-test scores, such as those generated by some Advanced Placement exams, were in many cases better predictors of student performance than scores from the multiple-choice SAT. Human judges were outperforming Scantron scoring machines when it came to predicting student success.

How could this be? The reason had to do with the undeniable importance of measurement format. What the test makers from ETS discovered was that *how* you measure something can be nearly as important as *what* you measure. In many universities, the vast majority of students' grades are based on essay exams. Few, if any, grades are derived from multiple-choice testing. And it turns out that the best way to predict how well someone will write essays in the future is to test them using an essay format today.

These findings should come as no surprise. Measurement format has been consistently shown to have a dramatic effect on results. In 2001, Yale University professor Robert Sternberg and his colleagues identified this phenomenon when they conducted a study with 324 participants, testing a variety of different abilities using both multiple-choice and essay-writing formats. They found that an individual's performance on one multiple-choice test tended to correlate with his or her performance on another multiple-choice test, regardless of what the two tests were trying to measure. In contrast, a person's performance on an essay exam showed a surprisingly weak correlation with performance on a multiple-choice exam, even when both tests were designed to measure the same subject.[6]

For instance, a student who did very well on an essay test about history did not necessarily do well on a multiple-choice test on history. But that same student, who excelled at writing essays, tended to do well on all the essay tests, whether they were about literature, science, or history. Apparently, people who are exceptional at writing essays are not necessarily good at answering multiple-choice questions. And vice versa.

So, if you want to predict how well students are going to perform at a college that will judge them using essays, you'd best test their academic aptitude using essays. In other words, in order to most accurately predict someone's performance, you must closely mimic the context in which the individual will have to perform.

This also holds true for the assessment of business executives, a point made clear by Professors Peter Bycio and June Hahn of Bowling Green State University, and management researcher Kenneth Alvares of Frito-Lay Inc.[7] They examined the results of 1,170 management candidates who were evaluated for their performance in areas including influencing people or organizational skills. Each skill area was assessed with both written tests and interviews. The researchers discovered that individuals' performances had more to do with *how* they were being tested than *what* they were being tested for.

Like Sternberg, Bycio and his colleagues found that individuals who excelled at taking written tests tended to do well in written exercises across all subjects. The same held true for those that did well at answering interview questions. These researchers concluded, "The exercise-specific ratings would be expected to correlate with job performance to the degree that the exercise involved accurately reflected the job itself."[8] In other words, the accuracy of any assessment tool is strongly influenced by how closely the tool's format mirrors the job itself.

So what does this mean when it comes to measuring Executive Intelligence? The vast majority of executives work in real-time verbal situations; that is, information is exchanged in conversations, questions are posed, and decisions are made on the fly. Multiple-choice questions, like those found on traditional intelligence measures, do a poor job of replicating this environment. The most valid tests of executive performance must mimic the job's real-time, verbal format; re-creating this is critical for any measure of Executive Intelligence. Interviews offer an excellent imitation of this setting. However, as mentioned previously, interviews have long been criticized as being inaccurate when it comes to assessing intelligence.

Human judges, critics assert, are believed to be highly unreliable. After all, the critics argue, how can human raters be as objective as multiple-choice scoring machines when it comes to measuring intelligence? But, it is a mistake to assume that humans cannot be objective.

Next time skeptics roll their eyes at relying upon human "subjectivity," remind them that they bet their life on human judgment every time they drive on a crowded freeway or when they agree to take a medicine prescribed by a doctor.[9] That's because when it comes to rendering judgments about many real-life situations, human expertise is unmatched.

In fact, studies have proven that human scorers can be highly consistent and accurate in their ratings. Extensive evidence supports the validity of PBI job interviews, for example. In those studies, the scores given by trained interviewers agreed to a very high degree on candidates, and their ratings have been proven to be highly predictive.[10] Still, most management scientists are resistant to introducing human graders into any test situation.

In fact, they would rather measure something of little importance without human intervention, than measure something of great importance by relying upon human observation. Consider the usefulness of relying upon machines to generate important information about a particular animal. Machines could easily determine the animal's weight, height, and length with great precision. However, this information would be far less important than knowing that the animal was actually a rhinoceros rather than a baby elephant. Only by human observation can we instantly realize what kind of animal it is, and that it is one best avoided rather than poked and prodded.

Obviously, when it comes to grading a multiple-choice exam, human judges will never be as precise as a Scantron machine. When it comes to evaluating interviews, however, human judges are unmatched. Because executives must apply their cognitive skills in real-time verbal situations, any measure of Executive Intelligence must use an interview format, and, research assures us that the judges who evaluate such interviews can be highly consistent and accurate.

There is an additional, critical reason why Executive Intelligence measures require an interview format: a conversation is the only way to expose and judge the cognitive skills a candidate uses to reach an answer. This is crucial, because a candidate's final answer to a question is not an adequate indicator of his or her level of Executive Intelligence. Rather, it is the process that led the person to their conclusion that reveals their strengths and weaknesses.

An algebra teacher cannot effectively evaluate the quality of a student's work without looking at the calculations that led to the final answer. Only by reviewing the student's intermediary steps can the teacher expose the deficiencies or strengths behind the solution. The same holds true for Executive Intelligence. The interviewer must delve into the intermediary steps the candidate used to reach the final answer, for it is the candidate's decision-making process that reveals his or her cognitive strengths and weaknesses. Only a human interviewer is capable of the probing dialogue that makes a candidate's thinking process explicit . . . and able to be evaluated.

# CHAPTER 14 SUMMARY

||||||||||||||||||||||||||

- Intelligence must be measured by methodologies that are totally distinct from those designed to measure knowledge.

- An intelligence question asks candidates to solve a new, unfamiliar problem using information made available to them, whereas knowledge questions merely require candidates to recall information.

- The cognitive skills that make up Executive Intelligence all represent activities that determine how well one *processes* the information available in order to render a sound conclusion.

- The format used to measure intelligence is crucial to the accuracy of the results, and it must closely mimic the context in which the skills will be used in real life. Therefore, Executive Intelligence must be measured in a verbal, real-time format that approximates the way that executive work is done.

- Human graders, such as those used in an interview format, are capable of rendering highly accurate and consistent findings. Using trained interviewers for an Executive Intelligence evaluation is a valid and necessary means of conducting the test.

# HOW DO YOU MEASURE EXECUTIVE INTELLIGENCE?

# CHAPTER 15

# Part One:
# Distinguishing Excellence

It is clear that we will never be able to identify the best business minds using only traditional methods, since none assess a candidate's level of Executive Intelligence. If the profound value of Executive Intelligence is to be finally recognized, we need a reliable means for assessing and comparing the capacities of real-life candidates. As has become clear, the only way to measure Executive Intelligence is to do so in a conversational format, one that uses a series of questions that measure the cognitive aptitudes identified as crucial to executive work.

Whether we are trying to discover executives' ability to accomplish tasks, work with other people, or evaluate and adapt their own thoughts and actions, an Executive Intelligence evaluation functions the same way. Using realistic work scenarios, the interviewer poses questions that call for the use of certain cognitive skills in order to solve problems. The questions do not cue the candidate to the cognitive aptitudes needed. Yet each question requires the application of specific skills if it is to be answered well.

For instance, a question designed to evaluate a person's ability to identify the flaws in the suggestions of other people would not directly prompt the candidate to do so. Instead, the candidate would be asked to analyze a situation and an appropriate response would identify the essential flaw in another person's suggestion. It is through this method that the candidate demonstrates an ability to actually perform the particular skill as he or she would on the job (i.e., without a prompt).

For each question, the candidate must analyze the situation, draw a conclusion, and justify their reasoning. During the examination, about five different scenarios are presented to the candidate, each of which serves as the basis for six or seven questions that are designed to measure a narrow set of cognitive skills. Through the use of multiple scenarios and more than thirty questions, a comprehensive measure of all of the cognitive skills of interest can be obtained. The entire interview requires about one hour to complete.

The interviewer uses pointed questions to explore the candidate's conclusions and the thinking that led to them. This type of questioning is what makes an Executive Intelligence measure unique. Candidates must solve problems in a real-time conversational setting, much as executives do on the job, and explain the reasoning for their actions. No question can be answered with a simple, "This is what I would do . . ." Instead, a candidate must explain "why" they would take a certain course of action. Through this exercise they reveal the quality of their thinking skills, which is, after all, at the heart of the Executive Intelligence evaluation.

It is not enough to simply score a candidate's final conclusions. Even though in the real world people are not generally required to make their thought processes this explicit, an Executive Intelligence interviewer has to probe the decision-making process during the assessment. There's no other way to fully evaluate a candidate's cognitive aptitudes—both their strengths and limitations.

## Executive Intelligence Assessment—Tasks

Let's take a look at an Executive Intelligence question about **task** accomplishment.

> QUESTION: *You are the CEO of a large software company. Your prices are being severely undercut by both domestic and foreign competitors. Your executive team recognizes a desperate need to cut costs. Your COO concludes that reducing labor costs through the outsourcing of most of your programming to foreign subcontractors is the answer. In fact, your COO has already received a number of proposals from service firms in both India and South Korea. What are some of the key questions about his proposal you'd like answered?*

> CANDIDATE ONE: Subcontractors almost always demand a large amount of money up front in order to secure payment and hire any additional personnel required to meet your needs. I need to know if we can *afford* this outlay.

> INTERVIEWER: *What do you mean by "afford"?*

> CANDIDATE ONE: Subcontractors sound tempting, but pursuing this option would be a waste of time if our company does not have the up-front money to pay for them. Our current operating budget exists for a reason, and if the financial burden of this initiative is going to paralyze our ability to spend on other essential priorities, like advertising and sales, then it doesn't make sense to pursue.

Here Candidate One is showing a poor ability to **critically examine underlying assumptions,** by failing to ask the essential question: Will outsourcing your programming lead to significantly lower overall costs? By focusing immediately on budgetary constraints, Candidate One overlooks a more central issue, namely, is the COO correct in his assumption that outsourcing this work is the answer to their cost problems? Further, in Candidate One's cost analysis he has failed to account for and **identify likely unintended consequences** of outsourcing and their associated costs, such as the difficulty of managing people from a long distance, working in a drastically different time zone, or the disruption caused by significantly downsizing the current labor force.

> INTERVIEWER: *What other questions might you want answered about your COO's proposal?*
>
> CANDIDATE ONE: **Are the subcontractors reliable?**
>
> INTERVIEWER: *What do you mean by "reliable"?*
>
> CANDIDATE ONE: **How often do they screw up? Are their mistakes going to slow my product launches? I'd want to get reliability and customer-satisfaction data from the various subcontractors and their customers.**

Here the candidate is showing a poor facility for **recognizing what is known about an issue and what more needs to be known.** He has created too narrow a scope for his inquiry by choosing to define reliability only in terms of subcontractor mistakes, rather than comparing the rate of the subcontractor mistakes to the current rate of his own in-house staff.

Overall, Candidate One has shown a poor aptitude for some of the key cognitive skills necessary to effectively complete executive **tasks**. This is of significant concern, since a large percentage of an executive's responsibilities center around his or her ability to analyze situations such as this, provide appropriate guidance to subordinates, and draw sound conclusions.

Let's take a look at a very different answer by Candidate Two:

CANDIDATE TWO: The first thing I need to know is why the COO has concluded that outsourcing our programming is the best answer to our cost problems. He may be right, but reducing our overall costs, not just our in-house labor costs, is our critical need. And while programmers are expensive, would replacing a large percentage of our team with foreign labor be necessarily less so? For instance, programming subcontractors would require massive upfront training about our products, market, and customer needs. We'd also become totally dependent on them for new product development, maintenance, and ongoing customer-service issues. In what ways will these costs affect the savings that outsourcing would bring?

Here we see Candidate Two displaying a high level of skill in **critically examining underlying assumptions.** She understands that the core assumption underlying her COO's conclusion needs to be confirmed (i.e., outsourcing automatically equals cheaper production). Candidate Two is also pointing out that there are other indirect costs (upfront investment, ongoing customer service, and software-development issues) that must be considered in the analysis. She is showing a high degree of skill in **recognizing what is known about an issue and what more needs to be known.**

INTERVIEWER: *What other questions would you like answered?*

CANDIDATE TWO: Well, couldn't total outsourcing of our programming cause a severe disruption in our labor force? What would be the costs of aggravated labor relations and the potential accompanying employee departures or even work stoppages? I don't know that much about software companies, but wouldn't our productivity be affected

by moving an essential part of our business to a geographically distant
workforce, operating in an entirely different time-zone?

Here we see Candidate Two effectively considering **likely unintended
consequences** of the COO's proposal, including aggravated labor relations and potential impairment to worker productivity.

Candidate Two would score very well on this portion of an Executive
Intelligence measure. She demonstrates a strong facility for some of the
essential cognitive aptitudes that determine leadership success. Few executives possess such proficiency, and it is these individuals who have the
capacity to be stars.

It is important to note that the candidate volunteered that she did
not have much knowledge about the scenario topic, the software industry. But that is one of the key attributes of an Executive-Intelligence
measure: only the most basic executive knowledge—and no industry expertise—is required to answer the question well.

Take, for instance, Candidates Two's response to the interviewer's inquiry "What other questions would you like answered?" She chose to
focus on labor and productivity disruptions. If, however, she had identified completely different reservations, such as protection of intellectual
property, or negative public reaction to exporting U.S. jobs, she would
still have scored just as well on the cognitive skill that deals with *anticipating unintended consequences.*

That is because scoring well on the measure has nothing to do with
which specific unintended consequences candidates select; it requires
only that they recognize that there are, in fact, likely unintended consequences to the COO's proposal. They demonstrate this by highlighting
one or two that are highly relevant. Again, it is not the candidates' knowledge that determines their facility for this test; it's their reasoning and the

cognitive skills behind it that we are seeking to measure. Only the most basic executive knowledge is needed for their answer.

There is no single right answer to any Executive Intelligence question. The measure concerns only the aptitude a candidate's answer displays regarding the cognitive skills being measured. All answers are considered, not in terms of what candidates know, but in terms of how skillfully they approach or use information to arrive at a sound response. This same principle holds true whether the cognitive skills involved fall into the category of tasks, people, or self.

# Executive Intelligence Assessment—People

Let's take a look at a different Executive Intelligence scenario, one that is focused on the cognitive skills that allow one to effectively work with and through other **people.**

> QUESTION: *You are the general manager of sales and marketing at Rinaldi Manufacturing. You have been with the company for only a year when Amanda, one of Rinaldi's senior account managers, asks to meet with you about concerns she has with the way her immediate superior, Rick, has been handling one of Rinaldi's customers. Rick is a senior vice president and reports directly to you. At Rinaldi it is always expected that employees respect the chain of command; they are to raise concerns with their immediate supervisors before bringing such issues to the attention of others. You know Amanda has not brought this issue up with Rick. What do you do?*

CANDIDATE ONE: I would contact Rick directly and let him know that Amanda has some concerns that Rick must address with her. I would also ask Rick what is going on between him and Amanda and whether or not he needs me to get more involved.

INTERVIEWER: *Why would you choose this course of action?*

CANDIDATE ONE: Well, this situation clearly needs to be worked out between Rick and Amanda. As a senior VP, Rick's got to find a way to handle these issues with his own team. And I need to be able to trust that my people can work such things out among themselves.

Candidate One's response shows that he poorly **anticipates the likely emotional reactions** of the participants. By directly approaching Rick with Amanda's comments, Candidate One risks intensifying a possible conflict between them. He also could be exposing Amanda to Rick's angry reaction without any warning, which she could view as a breach of trust. Moreover, Candidate One fails to recognize the **limitations of what he can and cannot conclude** from Amanda's request for a meeting. Based on her assertions and his short tenure with Rinaldi, he does not have sufficient information to know the nature of the problem, and he fails to seek clarification.

INTERVIEWER: *Are there further steps you'd take?*

CANDIDATE ONE: Just to be safe, I'd also ask around to see if anyone else has seen or heard of any problem with Rick or his customers.

INTERVIEWER: *Why would you take this additional step?*

CANDIDATE ONE: Because Rick may be part of the problem and may not have given me the full story. I would want to check with other people to make sure that I'm getting the truth.

Candidate One demonstrates a deficiency in **recognizing the probable effects** of his actions. While he acknowledges that Rick may not be objective enough to give reliable information about the situation, his plan to ask third parties for confirmation risks inadvertently raising questions about his senior VP's competence.

Candidate One shows an alarming lack of some of the essential cognitive skills that enable an executive to effectively manage **interpersonal** situations. Handling circumstances such as these are an essential component of any leader's responsibilities. They are often highly charged, and manifesting poor judgment can be catastrophic. In this instance, Candidate One is inadvertently risking alienating two of his key employees, without ensuring effective resolution of a potential problem with a Rinaldi customer. Even more important, these blunders jeopardize the confidence and trust his employees place in him. For instance, Amanda may choose to tell others that she had expected to have a confidential discussion with Candidate One, but that her trust had been betrayed. Or, Rick may hear that Candidate One has been indirectly "checking up on him." This could result in a breakdown in their relationship.

A candidate with better Executive Intelligence might respond in the following manner:

CANDIDATE TWO: While I know this is a break in protocol, I would meet with Amanda and find out her specific concerns.

INTERVIEWER: *Why would you choose to meet with her?*

CANDIDATE TWO: Well, it's very likely that Amanda's aware of the company policy regarding our chain of command, and the fact that she's chosen to disregard it suggests there may be a problem that requires my involvement. Also, the fact that it concerns one of our customers adds some urgency to the matter. Regardless, I'm pretty new to this company, so there's probably a lot I don't know. I'd definitely want to meet with her to find out more.

Here, Candidate Two effectively recognizes the **limitations of what he can and cannot conclude** from Amanda's request for a meeting. He realizes that he does not have sufficient information regarding what is happening with Rinaldi's customer, nor does he know why Amanda has chosen to disregard the chain of command.

> INTERVIEWER: *So what would you hope to find out from the meeting with Amanda?*
>
> CANDIDATE TWO: I'd need to find out what the nature of the customer problem is and why she chose to go over Rick's head with it. Amanda's refusal to bring this up directly with Rick may be due to some interpersonal conflict with him; but the customer problem might be so urgent that there's not enough time for Rick and Amanda to resolve any personal differences.
>
> If, however, Amanda does not have a very good reason for going over Rick's head, I would remind her that we have a chain of command and why it exists. It is essential that Amanda and Rick be able to trust each other. Resolving such conflicts privately with one another directly forms the basis of such trust. I would explain this and reinforce the importance of taking such issues up directly with Rick in the future. I would also assure her that I would not discuss this exchange with Rick to avoid complicating the situation further.

By meeting with Amanda to establish the nature of the customer problem, Candidate Two adeptly **recognizes and balances the needs of different**

**stakeholders**—Amanda and Rick, on the one hand, and one of Rinaldi's customers, on the other. Candidate Two also skillfully **recognizes the probable effects** of his actions. By meeting with Amanda, Candidate Two does allow her to break protocol; but if her behavior turns out to be inappropriate, he avoids encouraging such acts in the future by stressing the importance of the chain of command. Finally, Candidate Two recognizes Rick's **likely emotional reactions** to Amanda's bypassing his authority by promising to keep his conversation with Amanda in confidence.

Candidate Two's answer demonstrates an impressive amount of social savvy. It is important to note that his solutions involve the application of more than one cognitive ability. That is the hallmark of skillful executive behavior, which always involves the consideration of multiple factors in a complex situation.

This is similar to the way top poker players approach their game during any individual hand. They are simultaneously looking at the value of their own cards, looking for "tells" from their opponents, calculating their odds of winning, and judging how their behavior will affect their betting options as the game progresses. Overlooking any one of these factors could cause them to lose the hand. Like a world-class poker player, Candidate Two was simultaneously considering the customer's needs, Rick's and Amanda's interests, and their likely reactions to his choices of action. By doing this, the candidate was maximizing the probability of reaching a desirable outcome to a highly charged situation.

The responses of Candidates One and Two are by no means the only answers that could be given to this question. Another candidate might choose to meet with both Rick and Amanda together to clarify what is going on. During an Executive Intelligence measure, a candidate's reasoning and line of inquiry are judged for how likely they are to bring about a desirable outcome. This highlights the essential role of the skilled interviewer in guiding the process. Different candidates may choose different ways of addressing the same situation. And some of these solutions may be equally skilled. It requires a trained interviewer to explore the logic of each and determine the candidate's facility for the cognitive skills involved.

## Executive Intelligence Assessment—Self

The final category included in an Executive Intelligence measure is the cognitive skills involved in **self,** which refers to one's ability to evaluate and adapt one's own thinking and actions. Here is an example of a question designed to evaluate one's ability in this area.

> QUESTION: *You are competing for a big promotion to take over ship-ping operations for all of Camden Industries. Your main competition is a coworker named Mark, whom you've always seen as a bit of a show-boat. You are planning to suggest a new initiative that you believe will dramatically help Camden better anticipate changes in its market, and you hope this proposal will help differentiate you from Mark in the eyes of Camden's COO. You want to institute an ongoing analysis of chang-ing customer requirements by modifying the customer-satisfaction sur-vey; you want to ask if there are additional or upcoming needs that Camden's shipping department could possibly meet. At the weekly de-partment meeting with the COO, you wait for the ideal moment and then share your idea with the staff. When you finish, you are just begin-ning to enjoy supportive looks from some of your colleagues when Mark blurts out, "I bet most of those surveys never even get filled out. How useful is this exercise really gonna be?" Everyone turns back to you and waits for your response. What do you do?*

CANDIDATE ONE: I respond, "Mark, I'm not sure what our response rates are, but what are you basing your assertion on? Why don't we find out the facts first before we disregard this idea?"

INTERVIEWER: *Why would you choose to respond in this way?*

CANDIDATE ONE: Everyone is probably aware that Mark is acting aggressively and trying to make me look bad. Also, it's pretty clear that his criticism is just based on a guess. By calling Mark on it, I make clear that he's speculating and being unnecessarily negative.

By disregarding Mark's comment as speculative, and therefore baseless, Candidate One is failing to take a critical look at his **own biases or the limitations of his own perspective.** In reality, he doesn't know whether Mark is right or wrong about the survey response rates. Mark presents his critique antagonistically, but this does not make the substance of his argument invalid. Candidate One has allowed his reaction to Mark's style to distract him from the value in Mark's critique. He answers in an unproductive, defensive manner, and as a result, he cannot see how to use the substance of the criticism to **improve his own plan of action.**

INTERVIEWER: *Is there anything else you would add?*

CANDIDATE ONE: Well, I'd probably address Mark further, saying something like, "Mark, your criticisms are more of a distraction than a help. Let's try to be constructive."

INTERVIEWER: *Why would you say that?*

CANDIDATE ONE: To make sure that the benefit of my idea is not lost, and that everyone understood that Mark offered nothing of value to the discussion.

Candidate One is compounding the flaws of his initial response. Given the opportunity, he fails to **appropriately defend his idea** by more fully explaining its value and bringing the focus back to the idea itself. Instead, he concentrates on criticizing Mark and dismissing his comments.

The vast majority of executives have a difficult time looking critically at their own ideas, whether as a result of natural human tendency, temperament, or the conditioning that comes from working in a competitive environment. However, the best new ideas rarely emerge in perfect form. Executives must be able to absorb and use criticism to improve and clarify their ideas. They also must be able to distinguish between hollow criticism and valid criticism, separate from the form or tone with which it is presented. Regardless of how Candidate One felt about Mark's demeanor, the substance of his criticism may have been useful. Candidate One's poor skill in this category of Executive Intelligence prevented him from possibly improving his own idea.

Now let's take a look at how another candidate might answer the same question:

> CANDIDATE TWO: I would say, "Mark, you may be right that our survey response rate is too low for it to be a reliable source of information. This initiative is too important to rely upon bad data. Perhaps we can identify those customers who tend not to return the written surveys and make personal calls to them."

By immediately recognizing the usefulness of Mark's comments, Candidate Two demonstrates a strong capacity for **recognizing flaws in her own thinking.** She then very skillfully **takes corrective action** by following up with personal calls to unresponsive customers.

INTERVIEWER: *Is there anything else you would add?*

CANDIDATE TWO: Yes, ultimately Mark may be right that some customers don't respond to the surveys. But these forms are still the cheapest and easiest way for us to get the information we need. So it makes sense to use them wherever possible. And I would explain that to the group.

INTERVIEWER: *Why would you choose to handle it this way?*

CANDIDATE TWO: As much as Mark's style may irritate me, it's important not to lose focus on my idea and its potential merit, which is to get accurate information about changes in our customers' needs. Mark does raise an important question about the best way to go about doing that. But the idea itself remains worthwhile.

By reaffirming the essential value in her proposal, Candidate Two **appropriately defends the merit of her idea.** Finally, in distinguishing between Mark's aggressive style and the useful value of his statement, Candidate Two **confronts and manages her own biases,** so they do not blind her to improvements to her own plan.

The best executives demonstrate a facility for seeking out and using information or criticism that suggests a way of improving their own thinking or behavior. Candidate Two shows a strong capacity for the cognitive skills that allow this to happen. Many executives react with defensiveness to critical feedback. Others capitulate to criticism far too easily, causing them to abandon the essential merits of their ideas. It is the rare leader who is capable of turning the magnifying glass on himself or herself in order to recognize when criticisms are worth using and, *just as important,* to identify when such criticisms are baseless and he or she should stand fast. This is an essential capacity for any leader, because so many of the greatest and most important initiatives in history have been met with scathing criticism.

When Alexander Graham Bell attempted to sell his telephone technology, Western Union's president, William Orton, responded by asking, "What use could this company make of an electrical toy?"[1] Erasmus Wilson, a professor at Oxford University, commented, "When the Paris Exhibition closes, electric light will close with it and no more be heard of."[2] Decades later Kenneth Olsen, president and founder of Digital Equipment Corporation, said, "There is no reason for any individual to have a computer in their home."[3]

All of these statements seem humorous in retrospect, but at the time they echoed widely held criticisms of these new technologies. Only those purveyors of new technology who were capable of differentiating between substantive criticisms and baseless attacks were able to succeed. Today's leaders are confronted with similar challenges. They are constantly bombarded with multiple sources of critical feedback. Yet star leaders act appropriately, recognizing and adopting what is useful and ignoring what is unwarranted. The preceding interview question measures some of the skills that are most central to doing so.

# Part Two:
# Executive Intelligence—
# Validation Behind the Theory

||||||||||||||||||||||||

As you can see, none of the Executive Intelligence questions prompted the candidates to use any particular cognitive skill in their response, but the problems required the application of specific skills to answer them well. There is no one right solution to the hypothetical situations posed. Executive Intelligence measures focus on the quality of a candidate's thinking process and evaluate whether or not this process enabled him or her to reach a sound conclusion.

When someone provides a strong, well-reasoned answer to an Executive Intelligence question, their answer often seems obvious *after the fact*. This is because the skillful thinking behind it is so clear in its inescapable logic. But coming up with a strong response is very difficult. Skillful thinking is never easy, particularly in the on-demand environment of work that the test replicates.

Through this question-and-answer process, interviewers judge the quality of a candidate's responses and generate an Executive Intelligence score. These scores can be used to compare candidates. And that is the essential utility of an Executive Intelligence measure; it creates a standard for comparing executives and predicting their future performance.

Executive Intelligence questions are unique in terms of both their structure and their focus. They have been designed to accurately target the cognitive abilities crucial to executive performance in the three categories of **tasks,** other **people,** and **self.** But what is the evidence to support the contention that the Executive Intelligence assessment actually measures a unique type of intelligence?

In a study published in 2002 by the author of this book, a group of sixty-six professionals were assessed using: an Executive Intelligence instrument, PBI interviews, personality inventories, and a widely used IQ test. The Executive Intelligence scores were sufficiently correlated to the IQ scores as to suggest that both instruments were measuring a type of intelligence. However, the level of correlation established that the two instruments were measuring different, but slightly overlapping skills. In other words, the Executive Intelligence instrument was found to be a valid assessment of intelligence, but one that measured a different type of intelligence than that of IQ tests. What's more, the Executive Intelligence examination showed no significant correlation with either PBI or personality measures, suggesting that the information it provides is unique from that yielded by those commonly used tools.[4]

One burning question still remains: Does a person's performance on an Executive Intelligence measure actually allow us to predict their leadership ability in real life? In another study performed by the author of this book, thirty-five executives from different industries were interviewed and scored using an Executive Intelligence methodology. Anonymous performance ratings were then collected from peers, subordinates, and superiors for each candidate. Correlations between interview scores and the performance ratings demonstrated Executive Intelligence to be a very strong predictor of executive success (.41).[5]

In 2004, the Evaluation Center at Western Michigan University, a group that specializes in the evaluation of assessment instruments, re-

viewed all existing Executive Intelligence questions and their correspond-
ing answer keys, as well as the empirical findings collected to date. Led by
management professor Jennifer Palthe, the group concluded:

> "A review and examination of material and data associated with the Ex-I
> suggest that this instrument has significant potential as a managerial as-
> sessment tool. It is evident that it measures what it purports to measure
> and captures aspects of real-time managerial performance that other in-
> struments are unable to capture. The Ex-I clearly has construct, content,
> convergent, and face validity; its internal reliability reflects its dependabil-
> ity and precision as a measuring instrument; and initial evidence suggests
> strong criterion-related (concurrent) validity. Its ability to capture a
> manager's ability to reason deductively, to evaluate arguments, and to un-
> derstand meaning provides practitioners with a tool that can adequately
> identify potentially exceptional managerial performers. Furthermore, the
> instrument's practical relevance and ease-of-scoring makes it highly at-
> tractive as a superior, contemporary managerial assessment tool."[6]

To date, Executive Intelligence interviews have been administered to over
five hundred senior executives in eighteen different countries and in seven
different languages. Neither language, country of origin, gender, nor race has
demonstrated any influence on testing performance (see the appendix).

The most important contribution of the academic IQ test was its
measure of the universal cognitive skills essential to performance in
schools. Proficiency in solving arithmetic problems or in reading com-
prehension is predictive of school performance regardless of language or
national boundaries.

The same can be said about the Executive Intelligence measure. The
underlying thinking skills are universal, and an individual's aptitude for
them, in large part, determines his or her performance regardless of language or national origin. The ability to *critically evaluate assumptions,* for

instance, or to *recognize and balance the different needs of stakeholders* forms the basis of executive performance across different industries or continents. This is what makes an Executive Intelligence evaluation so useful. It provides us with a standardized method of comparing individuals from different companies, industries, or countries on the essential cognitive aptitudes of executive work.

The accuracy of the Executive Intelligence test has been repeatedly borne out in actual practice. For instance, in 2002, a billion-dollar company was seeking to replace its CEO. Several senior executives within the company were competing for the top spot. In order to obtain some objective, external perspective, highly trained consultants were hired to assess each candidate using PBI interviewers and very thorough reference checks. The assessment results elevated one of the candidates to the top of the list. As a final verification, he was sent for an Executive Intelligence evaluation, which revealed a prominent weakness. Though none of the references had mentioned this, the candidate was particularly weak at recognizing and correcting errors in his own judgment. He had a strong tendency to "dig in his heels" even when he knew he was wrong. In Executive Intelligence terms, he was severely lacking in the category of **self.**

The assessment team gathered and presented their findings to the candidate. After a review of his relevant strengths, he was informed that the assessment results revealed an essential weakness. When confronted with the particulars of his deficiency, he sat stunned and remained silent for several moments. Finally, he said, "How did you know? This has always been my Achilles' heel. *Who told you this?*" The Executive Intelligence interviewer responded, "The results of your test showed a consistent pattern." To which the candidate replied, "I've hidden this from my bosses for years, but I've been privately seeing an executive coach for this very issue." While such dramatic confessionals are not common, the Executive Intelligence measure consistently provides invaluable insights regarding a leader's capacities.

# CHAPTER 15 SUMMARY

||||||||||||||||||||||||||

- An Executive Intelligence evaluation utilizes realistic work scenarios posed by a trained interviewer.

- None of the questions cue the candidate to the cognitive aptitudes needed to answer them, but each requires the use of these skills if the questions are to be answered well.

- For each question the candidate must analyze the situation, draw a conclusion, and justify his or her reasoning.

- Through the use of multiple scenarios and questions, a comprehensive measure of all of the cognitive skills of interest can be achieved.

- Executive Intelligence scores are not simply based on a candidate's final answer, but also on the thought processes that led to his or her conclusion.

- The information provided by an Executive Intelligence measure is distinct from that yielded from other commonly used assessment tools, such as: PBIs, IQ tests, or personality measures.

- Research has proven Executive Intelligence scores to be highly predictive of executive success.

# CHAPTER 16

# Teaching and Developing
# Executive Intelligence

||||||||||||||||||||||||||

Can Executive Intelligence be taught? Absolutely. Like any set of skills, it can be learned, practiced, and improved. Even though extensive research suggests that genetic influences determine roughly 50 percent of an individual's intellectual capacity, that still leaves a large amount that can be improved upon. And there is evidence that training in better thinking skills can have considerable lasting, positive effects.

In the most impressive empirical study to date on improving cognitive abilities, Harvard University professor Richard Hernstein and several colleagues conducted a year-long study with 895 seventh-grade Venezuelan students.[1] In order to establish baseline skills, the students were tested with a broad series of commonly used measures of IQ, including the Otis-Lennon School Ability Test (OLSAT) and the General Abilities Test (GAT). The students were then divided into two groups that were essentially equivalent in their IQ test scores.

One group, designated "control," was instructed in the standard academic curriculum. The other group, designated "experimental," was taught the standard curriculum, *plus* they were provided with additional courses designed to develop their faculties for reasoning, problem solving, and decision-making. Professor Hernstein described the supplemental training: "The focus was on cognitive skills that apply to learning and intellectual performance independently of subject matter, rather than conventional academic content."[2] In other words, Hernstein concentrated on teaching kids how to think. This special course encouraged dramatically more interaction between teacher and student. Rather than the traditional passive classroom role, the students in the experimental group were encouraged to give continual feedback to the teacher. They were much more involved with the flow of material, which was presented as part of an interactive conversation rather than a lecture.

After the year of instruction, both groups were tested again for their cognitive skills. On average, the *experimental* group's "post-training" percentile scores increased dramatically, while the *control* group's scores remained largely unchanged. For instance, students in the *control* group who began with a score in the 50th percentile remained in the 50th percentile when they retook the tests. However, a student in the *experimental* group who started with a matching 50th percentile score, improved to the 64th percentile after receiving the special training. These dramatic results were found across the battery of tests, regardless of subject—verbal, math, or reasoning.

A second study conducted by Professors Tim van Gelder and Melanie Bissett of the University of Melbourne and Professor Geoff Cumming of Le Trobe University gave 146 students a semester-long course specifically designed to improve their thinking skills.[3] During a series of problem-solving exercises, each student was given tailored guidance and feedback along each step of their decision-making process. After receiving this specialized instruction, almost all the students showed a marked improvement in their thinking skills. In fact, those students performing at the 50th percentile on standardized tests at the beginning of the course had improved their performance to the 79th percentile by the end of the course.

In general, it is clear that while genetic makeup certainly has something to do with intelligence, most individuals are not functioning at anywhere near their "intellectual ceilings." And as these studies demonstrate, with proper training, there is plenty of room for improvement before most people reach their cognitive limits. But why, if methods exist to improve cognitive skills, are the vast majority of highly educated executives falling far short in this area? One answer lies in traditional teaching methods that do little to develop skillful thinking.

From a young age, students are taught subject knowledge, not thinking skills. Abundant research shows that most classroom questions call for little more than the retrieval of content. In other words, throughout students' most important formative years of cognitive development, nearly all attention is given to memorizing "the facts." Although numerous studies have shown that reasoning can improve with appropriate instruction, students are seldom challenged to really think.[4]

In a typical exchange between a high school history teacher and his students, the instructor may ask: "What were the key events leading up to the American Revolutionary War, and when did they occur?" Students who respond with "the Stamp Act in 1765," or "the Townshend Acts of 1767," or "the Boston Tea Party of 1773," would elicit praise. A common follow-up question could be, "What exactly was the Stamp Act?" Again students would be applauded for their command of the facts, such as, "It was instituted in November of 1765 and required every newspaper, pamphlet, and other public or legal document in the colonies to display a British Stamp or Seal. To get these stamps you had to pay money."

An exchange that challenges the students' thinking skills would require a different approach, however. A teacher focused on developing cognitive skills might ask students the same initial question—"What were the key events leading up to the Revolutionary War?"—but follow-up questions would likely be much more thought-provoking, such as, "What do all these events have in common?" or "How did these events affect the form that the U.S. government eventually took?"

Certainly, knowledge about subjects like history, English, or chemistry is important, but teaching content alone does not provide people with the broad, general thinking skills essential to real-life work.[5] For example, while memorization of the periodic table may save a chemist from having to look up this information while on the job, it is only the thoughtful and creative application of that material that allows that same scientist to generate profound new research.

What is more, traditional classroom practices tend to exacerbate the problem of training students to solely memorize content rather than teach them how to skillfully process that information. Studies have shown that teachers typically give students little time to answer a question before providing an answer or turning to another pupil.[6] This practice discourages participants from engaging in reflective thought, which is essential to developing skilled thinking. Students who have to respond quickly to a question have little opportunity to display more than a rote recitation of knowledge. Interestingly, research shows that giving students just a little more time to answer makes a marked difference, both in their thoughtfulness and in the whole intellectual atmosphere of the classroom. As a result, individuals benefit from deeper insights and fuller understanding of the subjects being studied.[7]

Lurita Doan, CEO of New Technology Management, explains how success in today's school system has little to do with one's facility for skilled thinking:

> "Why is it that so often the valedictorian of the class can't translate that success in school to success in corporate leadership? In fact, it seems to be rarely the case. This is because getting an A in class has little to do with your ability to think. The 'A' student is the one that is best able to recite back what the teacher is saying. That shows the teacher, 'This student really understands what I'm saying. She's demonstrated that she's

absorbed what I'm teaching.' But all the student has done is regurgitate what they've been told. In business, you're almost always in uncharted territory and must be capable of thinking for yourself."

Unfortunately, by adulthood, few people have received any such training. Despite years of schooling they have not developed the thinking skills they need on the job. In fact, quite the opposite has occurred. Over time individuals have been conditioned to respond with immediate answers, relying exclusively on what they have memorized. Upon entering the workplace, they find themselves ill prepared to confront the complex, constantly changing circumstances that surround them. It's like someone who has practiced every day to run a marathon and then gets to the starting line only to discover that the event is a stock car race.

Teaching people how to think more skillfully requires time, effort, and determination. Students must be forced to do more than simply recite facts. California State University–San Bernardino psychology professor Diane Halpern, after extensive research into this phenomenon, discussed just how difficult this can be. "Beliefs that have been constructed over many years and the habits of mind that developed along with them will take multiple learning experiences, distributed over time and settings, before they will be successfully replaced with new ways of thinking and knowing about the world."[8]

Dick Parsons, CEO of Time Warner, who also holds a law degree, suggests that legal training may hold some of the answers regarding how to improve thinking skills:

"Law school training is different from business school and other types of professional education. The focus is on how to think in ways that allow you to attack complicated problems and break them down into manageable, solvable units. This gives you the ability to really understand something, even if at first it seems overwhelming. And that technique is not just useful in law but in business as well, because in business, problems are often multilayered and multidimensional. Law school training helps you to improve the thinking skills that help you to solve such problems."

Any law student will tell you that their first year in school was by far the most difficult because they were forced to approach problems in a brand-new way. Similarly, the goal of teaching Executive Intelligence is to help people break the deeply ingrained thinking habits that they have developed throughout their life. Improving one's Executive Intelligence is a demanding and ongoing process, and it requires participation in active, intense discussions.

The most effective means to accomplish this is indeed similar to the Socratic Method used in law schools, a format in which every participant in the dialogue can be called upon at any moment to critique a previous comment or advance the discussion to the next level. This cycle of articulation and critique helps students reflect on the issues—and that is how they learn cognitive skills. The more an individual is compelled to verbalize and reflect on their own thinking in response to the criticisms of others, the more that person will gain from the process.

Stephen Kaufman, a current senior lecturer at Harvard Business School and former CEO of Arrow Electronics, explains:

"When it comes to developing thinking skills, you have to do it through discussion rather than lecturing. In a discussion format people can be prodded to reason through things out loud. And they must be able to practice and make mistakes in a safe environment.

Many people believe that the only way to improve your skills is by making your own mistakes on the job. But this is a regrettable conclusion, because it assumes that no teaching format can be used to reduce mistakes by improving the skill with which people make their decisions. And this simply isn't the case."

So what might an Executive Intelligence learning exercise look like? In some ways it would resemble the Executive Intelligence assessment process, which relies upon the analysis of specially constructed workplace scenarios. A moderator—ideally a highly skilled thinker—would present a realistic problem and then initiate a dialogue designed to elicit responses from the participants. Because so much of the value of the exercise comes from active participation by the students, a small group, ideally no more than five people, is required. The moderator must be free to call on anyone to respond at any point in the discussion. This forces the students to stay engaged at all times, in order to avoid falling behind or becoming lost. Such intensive concentration is necessary to build up cognitive skills, just as targeted physical exercise is required to build up a muscle in the body.

Take a scenario designed to improve some of the essential cognitive skills regarding other people, one that specifically exercises *probable effects of particular actions* and *likely emotional reactions*.

A moderator might present the following scenario:

You are president of a market-research firm and you are presenting the findings of an in-depth analysis on a client's new product to the company's CEO and executive team. As you begin your presentation, the client CEO notices a mistake in the report summary handout. It is repeated throughout the report, and it is certainly something you or your team should have caught. Thankfully, the error is fairly minor, and does not affect any of the conclusions in the report.

You apologize for the mistake, take responsibility, but assure your client that the findings and all the substantive discussion points remain unchanged, and you proceed with your presentation.

A few minutes later, as the group is following along in the handout, the same mistake occurs again, and the CEO comments with annoyance, "Here it is again," as he shakes his head and looks at the rest of his team.

Again you apologize and point out that the typo is the same as the previous one, and that it will repeat several times throughout the report. But once more you stress that though regrettable, it does not affect the conclusions in the report or the substance of the day's discussion.

As you proceed with your presentation, you notice the CEO is leafing forward through the report, shaking his head and pointing out the repeated mistake to those sitting next to him. What do you do?

The moderator turns to a student and says, "Jerry, what would you do in this circumstance?"

Jerry responds, "Well, I'd ignore the interruption and keep going with my presentation. Hopefully his distractions will pass, and we could move on."

Moderator: "Why would you choose that course of action?"

Jerry: "He's just pissed off right now. It won't last. As a consultant you have to be able to bear such uncomfortable moments."

Recognizing that Jerry has failed to anticipate the *likely emotional reactions* of individuals based on what has already happened, the moderator responds, "Jerry, you've already acknowledged the mistake twice and apologized. Yet the CEO seems increasingly irritated. How likely is it that this will quickly pass?"

The moderator turns to another student and says, "Denise, what do you think of Jerry's approach and would you do the same?"

Denise responds, "I think Jerry is hoping for reasonable behavior from someone who has already demonstrated that they are likely to be unreasonable and has ratcheted up their distractive behavior. Instead, I would suggest to the group that we adjourn and reschedule the meeting so that we can correct the error in the report and begin again."

The moderator sees that Denise has moved the analysis forward, but in doing so has created another problem by failing to *consider the probable effects* of her solution. The moderator explains: "That's an interesting observation, Denise. I think we have to assume that the CEO's escalation in behavior means you probably can't ignore it and assume it will go away. Your choice of responding directly to the distraction seems appropriate. However, why would you suggest adjourning?"

Denise: "Well, the mistake has become a serious distraction. It makes more sense to eliminate it so that the group can focus and get the job done."

Moderator: "Indeed the meeting is currently being seriously disrupted. However, is adjourning absolutely necessary and is there any problem with that?"

The moderator turns to another student and asks, "Richard, what do you think of Denise's approach?"

Richard: "Well, it seems right to do something to prevent an ongoing distraction. But adjourning would delay getting the client the findings they need, and that could still be avoided. Instead, I think I would turn to the CEO and say, 'I am very sorry that this mistake occurred. It has become a significant distraction. We can reschedule this meeting for another time in order to correct the mistake. But seeing as it does not alter what we're here to talk about, would you all be willing to overlook it so that we can take advantage of this opportunity to get you the information you need?' "

Richard has articulated a skillful way of handling this complex interpersonal situation. Using the insights gleaned from the exchanges between his fellow students and the moderator, he was able to arrive at a solution that maximizes his chances of success in this scenario. The situation was crafted to require the use of a narrow set of cognitive skills. This ensures that the students are practicing these particular skills as they struggle their way to an ideal solution. By giving the students the opportunity to explain the shortcomings of their peers' thinking and improve upon it, they receive multiple opportunities to practice these skills.

It is said that the best way to truly grasp a subject is to teach it to others. This is because effective teaching requires an ability to clearly communicate issues as well as the capacity to identify and correct misunderstandings. By requiring that each student critique the previous answer, all are given an opportunity to serve as both teacher and student.

But most important, each is forced to actively struggle with the limitations in his or her own thinking and the challenges of identifying the weaknesses in the thinking of others. Over time, students become more adept at these activities, which ultimately sharpens their Executive Intelligence.

These exercises require significant concentration and hard work on the part of both moderator and participants, but through such efforts one can increase their cognitive skills, and that benefits more than just the individuals involved. As was discussed earlier in this book, it is imperative that businesses populate their ranks using people possessing high executive intelligence. Further, those with exceptional Executive Intelligence can only function at their peak when surrounded by others with a similar level of skill. So, when a sufficient number of employees participate in these training exercises, it serves to popularize a habit of constructive dialogue, a behavior that is at the heart of Executive Intelligence and therefore can be modeled and passed on to other individuals throughout an organization. Ultimately, this dissemination helps to elevate the quality of decision-making throughout a workforce. As we will see, such practices can help organizations guard against a nearly universal slide toward mediocrity and decay.

# CHAPTER 16 SUMMARY

||||||||||||||||||||||||||

- The cognitive abilities that comprise Executive Intelligence can be learned, practiced, and improved.

- Research has proven that thinking skills can be dramatically increased through specialized instruction that provides students with tailored guidance and feedback along each step of their decision-making process.

- Learning how to think more skillfully requires time, determination, and effort because it goes against habits that have been established and reinforced by years of schooling.

- Executive Intelligence is best taught using a Socratic method not unlike that used in law schools. It calls for a small-group environment and a trained facilitator.

- The payoff from improving an individual's thinking skills can have a profound, positive effect on his or her coworkers and the organization as a whole.

# CHAPTER 17

# Valuing Executive Intelligence

An iron-man triathlon starts with a 2.4-mile swim, continues with a 112-mile bicycle race, and finishes with a 26.2-mile run. No matter how strong a swimmer an individual is, they will still lose the race if they are terrible cyclists or slow runners. So when athletes train for a triathlon, it makes no sense for those who are already exceptional at swimming, but unskilled at cycling or running, to spend most of their training time in the pool. They may improve their swim time by a small increment, but their weakness in the other events will still cause them to lose the race. And when predicting who is most likely to win the race, it makes little sense to look just at an individual's swim times.

Yet management scientists have been using their stopwatches to time only a single component of job performance: knowledge. In terms of the triathlon example, they thought they were measuring someone's overall athletic ability, when in actuality they were simply measuring swimming skill. And while being a good swimmer is relevant to winning a triathlon, it doesn't take into account the other portions of the race. Similarly, while knowledge is one important component of executive performance, it is hardly all that is needed. Intelligence plays an equally important role in business success. Ignoring intelligence has rendered our evaluation and training efforts unfocused and incomplete.

This book has attempted to break down executive "athleticism" into its component parts, focusing on a fundamental set of skills that has been completely neglected up to now. By building upon one of the most profound discoveries of management science—that cognitive aptitude (or intelligence) has enormous influence on managerial capability—we can give Executive Intelligence the attention it deserves and in the process capitalize on its value.

Like other businessmen, management scientists must identify and create new and exciting products for their customers to buy. But in this zeal to churn out new wares, they've failed to notice the distinction between knowledge and intelligence. As a result their services have emphasized knowledge alone, both in assessments and training. By committing all their energy to measuring and developing knowledge, management scientists have essentially been spending all their time in the pool. But no matter how extensive an executive's knowledge, that expertise is of little value without the underlying aptitudes (intelligence) to skillfully apply it. The point is not to stop valuing knowledge, but rather to start valuing intelligence as well.

Academic intelligence has been proven for nearly a century to have a substantial impact on managerial success. Undeniably, cognitive skills explain in large part how good an executive will be. Yet, until now, no one had come up with a theory of intelligence that was specific to business. As a result, there has been no way to evaluate or develop the cognitive skills that most directly affect leadership. Now, with the recognition of Executive Intelligence, we finally have a means of ensuring that those people who have decision-making responsibilities within organizations will be skilled enough to make those decisions well.

Executive Intelligence is not just a tool to assess people. The skills that comprise it are crucial to an organization's success and must be instilled into a company's personnel at every level through an ongoing, concerted effort, in hiring, promoting, and training. We have come to take these cognitive skills for granted, assuming that executives are already proficient in them and that they will remain so throughout their careers. But this assumption is simply untrue; too many executives are not skilled in these areas and, without rigorous practice, will remain so. Further, over time people's cognitive skills can become eroded if they are not exercised regularly. To ensure that the overall level of intelligent behavior in an organization goes up rather than down, we must cultivate Executive Intelligence in ourselves and in our people. The payoff can be enormous: it can mean the difference between an organization that thrives and one that dies.

Organizations have been compared to living organisms that experience cycles of growth, aging, and then decline that eventually ends their existence.[1] This pattern has been viewed as inevitable as death and taxes. But organizational decay is not inevitable. Certainly every company goes through difficult times, sometimes for a month, sometimes for a year, or even longer. If these troubles are drastic enough, they can kill off a corporation. But while every company stumbles at some point, these struggles do not necessarily have to result in organizational decline. Obstacles can be overcome and tough periods minimized. The dynamics that cause companies to fail can be interrupted or prevented entirely. Unlike a living organism's life cycle, there is nothing predetermined about the deterioration of businesses.

It is a truism of management literature that an organization's success is dependent on the quality of its people. So, more than any other factor, a business's decline or failure comes as a result of the diminution in quality of those people.

Stephen Kaufman, former of CEO of Arrow Electronics, expands on this idea:

> "The central difficulty that comes from organizations' growth is that, by and large, as they get bigger they tend to slide into mediocrity. This

is because it is extremely hard to find and keep talented people. They are just too rare.

So when it comes to hiring enough people to fill five hundred openings, the vast majority of them are inevitably not going to be 'A' players. And this is how you begin your slide. The often-stated cliché is true: ' "A" players hire "A" players, but "B" players hire "C" players.' This is how, over time, organizations get stacked in the middle with B and C players. Most of these people simply don't have the skill level to take you where you need to go, and important things are being done by people that are operating outside of their capability boundaries. The problem is that these less skilled employees exist in such large numbers, and are in so many different parts of the company, that they start to have a lot of influence over the core behavior of your organization."

Kaufman helps illuminate why so many companies struggle with mediocrity as they grow. But once you recognize the tendency for employee quality to slide, tangible steps can be taken to prevent it. Decline is not inevitable, Kaufman suggests, if a way can be found to maintain a high level of talent in your workforce.

Church & Dwight (C&D), one of oldest corporations still in existence, is an example in point. Founded in 1846, C&D has a diverse product line including Arm & Hammer baking soda, toothpaste, detergents, and commercial-cleaning and pet products. But this landmark institution ran into serious trouble during the early 1990s, when the company apparently lost its facility for consistent smart decision-making.

Bob Davies, the CEO of Church & Dwight since 1995, recollects:

"About fifteen years ago, in the early 1990s, C&D started getting into serious trouble. Their laundry detergent sales had started to decline due to significant product advances introduced by some of their main competitors. This problem arose simultaneously with significant declines in the sales of one of C&D's most aggressively growing product lines, Arm & Hammer toothpaste. The drop in sales involving both our detergents and toothpastes led total company sales to actually decline modestly in '93 and '94, and profits plummeted. C&D's stock followed, going from $32 a share, to $19.

Although I had spent a large portion of my career at C&D, starting there in 1969, I had left to pursue other interests in 1984. So when the troubles began, I was asked to come back as a consultant in order to help identify what had gone so wrong.

I still remember coming in that January morning. I noticed a huge rock, a piece of granite, that I can see even now outside of my office window. It had a bronze plaque carved in it with a vision statement about the importance of 'quality.' It was a little hard to understand, pretty high-minded stuff. It turned out it came from a consultant named Philip Crosby, who had written a book called *Quality Is Free*. The joke around here became 'Quality is free, but Crosby certainly is not.'

So when I saw this monument and heard about C&D's use of an outside consultant, I figured that the company must have done some fine work on improving product quality. But they had made so many poor decisions, I began to wonder where the quality control had been on the *decisions* the company had made, which is, after all, the most fundamental determinant of a business's success.

Here's an example. One of the reasons C&D was doing so well at the start of the 1990s was because of the success of its new line of baking soda toothpastes, which had been introduced in 1988. The paste was an instant success, but there was no major competition except for Colgate's baking soda toothpaste introduced in the early 1990s. By 1992, C&D's Arm & Hammer Brand toothpaste had captured 10 percent of America's $1.6 billion toothpaste market—it was C&D's hottest product. But in

1993, a whole bunch of other baking soda brands came out to compete. And that's when C&D's toothpaste sales really took a dive.

I wondered why C&D was so unprepared for the competition, and I was shocked to discover that they had just assumed that because their baking soda toothpaste was doing so well versus their only competitor, Colgate, that the baking soda segment was totally owned by C&D. As a result of this assumption that their growing market share in the toothpaste business was unstoppable, they had built a very expensive infrastructure around it, all of which they justified by the huge profitability coming from their expanding toothpaste sales.

Then all of a sudden, in 1993, a tremendous number of competing toothpastes were introduced with baking soda as a primary ingredient. And unlike Colgate, these new rivals, particularly Mentadent, were doing innovative things that caused an immediate market shift away from C&D's product. C&D had just assumed that because of Colgate's only modest level of success that no one else would be interested in getting into this market.

But it turns out that what was keeping others out had nothing to do with lack of interest. It was purely because all possible baking soda formulations had been patented by only two companies: C&D and Colgate. And guess what year Colgate's patents expired—1993.

I was baffled by C&D's failure to anticipate such a predictable, massive change in the market for one of its core products. This was only one of several immense oversights that could have seriously challenged C&D's 150 years of independent existence.

It became quickly clear that there was a systemic problem throughout the company. They had lost the fundamental strength that had kept them thriving for 150 years—sharp, sound decision-making.

I am a huge believer in intellectual rigor. A favorite movie of mine is *Twelve Angry Men* with Henry Fonda. You may remember that in this movie eleven members of a jury wanted to convict a young boy for murder after only ten minutes of deliberation. Only one man, Henry Fonda's character, insisted that they not jump to such a conclusion without a more rigorous analysis of the evidence. As they began to study and review the facts, they began to realize that it was unlikely that the boy was involved in the crime at all.

When I was asked to come back as C&D's CEO, the first thing I set about doing was bringing back the decision-making rigor that had been lost. I believe intensely in humbling oneself to the problem at hand and working through to a solution. I think that if you have good minds that work hard enough to get to the truth through rigorous analysis and active debate—that produces good decisions. But you have to keep practicing and reinforcing this if a company is to stay sharp. That's the antidote to what went so wrong with C&D."

Bob Davies found that the answer to C&D's problem was to restore a corporate environment that demanded its people elevate their reasoning and decision-making rigor. This requires ongoing effort if an organization is to continue to function at a high level. But if it makes such effort, its best years can occur during any period of its existence. A testament to this is the fact that over nearly a decade, between 1995 and 2004, C&D has entered one of the most profitable periods in its 150-year history and has outperformed the S&P 500 by nearly triple.

The events at C&D illustrate that the life cycle of a company is not predetermined; it can continue to thrive by keeping or restoring a culture that demands sound decision-making. But maintaining such an environment is not easy. In fact, extraordinary success can make such efforts even harder. Success tends to breed complacency, and that can allow even the best leader or organization to slide into mediocrity.

Jim Kilts, one of the world's most lauded and respected CEOs, describes how success can work against you:

> "Because I've been pretty successful, people will give me the benefit of the doubt even when I blow some smoke. Once you've achieved a certain track record, or have a certain reputation, people start thinking everything you say is right. They stop challenging you. But you have to force yourself and those around you to stay disciplined and keep testing the merits of what you say, because sloppiness can easily become a habit.
>
> Without the honest input of others you end up running an organization based too much on your past successes. You can't just go off what's worked in the past. This is how organizations get stagnant and complacent. To guard against this, I use an objective evaluation process, a very disciplined approach that demands frank and constructive feedback from my colleagues."

What Kilts is saying is that leaders must maintain systems that constantly challenge their thinking. As we gain experience, we all have a tendency to rely more and more on the lessons of our past. Seasoned executives, for example, often believe that they have already "seen it all," and that what worked in the past will continue to work. But the point at which they stop thinking and simply start applying rote knowledge to their job is where troubles really begin. As Kilts points out, one must remain humble and always examine what's really happening with fresh eyes, analytic rigor, and valuing the frank input of colleagues. A leader must continue to figure things out; in other words, they must always exercise their Executive Intelligence.

# Appendix

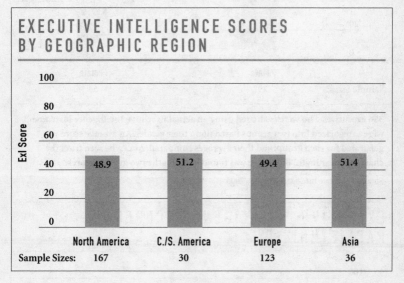

**EXECUTIVE INTELLIGENCE SCORES BY GEOGRAPHIC REGION**

| | North America | C./S. America | Europe | Asia |
|---|---|---|---|---|
| ExI Score | 48.9 | 51.2 | 49.4 | 51.4 |
| Sample Sizes: | 167 | 30 | 123 | 36 |

356 executives who were evaluated using an actual Executive Intelligence instrument were categorized into four groups based upon the geographic region in which they lived. An average score was generated for each geographic group, and group averages were compared. As can be seen from the chart, no meaningful difference was found between the groups' scores.

Source: Executive Intelligence Group, 2005

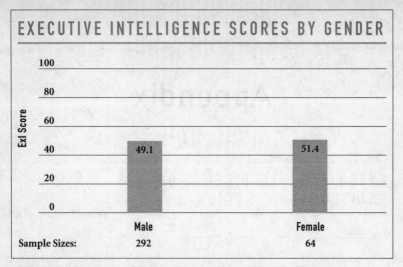

## EXECUTIVE INTELLIGENCE SCORES BY GENDER

**Exl Score**

| | Male | Female |
|---|---|---|
| | 49.1 | 51.4 |
| Sample Sizes: | 292 | 64 |

356 executives who were evaluated using an actual Executive Intelligence instrument were categorized into two groups based upon their gender. An average score was generated for each group, and their averages compared. As can be seen from the chart, no meaningful difference was found between the two groups' scores.

Source: Executive Intelligence Group, 2005

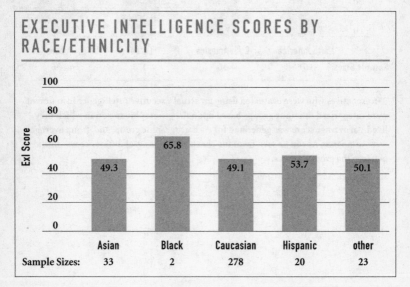

## EXECUTIVE INTELLIGENCE SCORES BY RACE/ETHNICITY

**Exl Score**

| | Asian | Black | Caucasian | Hispanic | other |
|---|---|---|---|---|---|
| | 49.3 | 65.8 | 49.1 | 53.7 | 50.1 |
| Sample Sizes: | 33 | 2 | 278 | 20 | 23 |

356 executives who were evaluated using an actual Executive Intelligence instrument were categorized into five groups based upon their race. An average score was generated for each group, and their averages compared. As can be seen from the chart, no meaningful difference was found between the groups' average scores.

Source: Executive Intelligence Group, 2005

# Notes

## The Beginning

1. Katrina Brooker, "Jim Kilts Is an Old-School Curmudgeon," *Fortune*, December 30, 2002, p. 3.

## What Every Business Needs

1. Jim Collins, *Good to Great* (HarperBusiness, 2001).

2. Jack Welch with John Bryne, *Straight from the Gut* (Warner Books, 2001).

3. Peter Drucker, *Managing in the Next Society* (Truman Talley Books, 2002).

## Where Things Went Wrong

1. Frank Schmidt and John Hunter, "The Validity and Utility of Selection Methods in Personnel Psychology: Practical and Theoretical Implications of 85 Years of Research Findings," *Psychological Bulletin*, 124, no. 2 (1998): pp. 262–274.

2. Frank Schmidt and John Hunter, "General Mental Ability in the World of Work: Occupational Attainment and Job Performance," *Journal of Personality and Social Psychology*, 86, no. 1 (2004): pp. 162–173.

3. John Hunter and Ronda Hunter, "Validity and Utility of Alternate Predictors of Job Performance," *Psychological Bulletin*, 96, no. 1 (July 1984): pp. 72–98.

4. Ken Richardson, *The Making of Intelligence* (Columbia University Press, 2000).

5. Peter Drucker, *Managing in the Next Society* (Truman Talley Books, 2002).

## Chapter 1

1. Justice Potter Stewart, U.S. Supreme Court, *Jacobellis v. Ohio*, 378 U.S. 184 (1964).

2. Quinn Spitzer and Ron Evans, *Heads You Win* (Simon and Schuster, 1997): Alex Taylor III, "Finally GM Is Looking Good," *Fortune*, 3/18/2002.

3. Sydney Finkelstein, *Why Smart Executives Fail* (Penguin Publishing, 2003).

4. Michael Scriven, *Reasoning* (McGraw-Hill Books, 1976).

5. http://seattlepi.nwsource.com/business/199821_sears16.html

6. http://www.mindfully.org/Industry/2005/Boeing-Michael-Sears18feb05.htm

7. http://www.pbs.org/newshour/updates/boeing12-01-03.html

8. Stanley Holmes, "Boeing, What Really Happened," *BusinessWeek*, December 15, 2003; "Worst Managers of 2003," *BusinessWeek*, January 12, 2004; Chuck Taylor, "Bad News Boeing," *Seattle Weekly*, 12/3/03; Julie Creswell, "Boeing Plays Defense," *Fortune*, 4/5/04.

9. Sydney Finkelstein, *Why Smart Executives Fail* (Penguin, 2003).

10. Geoffry Colvin, "How Rubbermaid Managed to Fail," *Fortune*, November 23, 1998.

## Chapter 2

1. Quinn Spitzer and Ron Evans, *Heads You Win* (Simon and Schuster, 1997).

2. Quinn Spitzer and Ron Evans, *Heads You Win* (Simon and Schuster, 1997).

3. Quinn Spitzer and Ron Evans, *Heads You Win* (Simon and Schuster, 1997).

4. Alec Fisher and Michael Scriven, *Critical Thinking* (Edgepress, 1997).

5. Segway press release, December 2001, http://www.segway.com/aboutus/press_releases/pr_120301.html.

6. Alec Fisher and Michael Scriven, *Critical Thinking* (Edgepress, 1997).

## Chapter 3

1. N.J. Mackintosh, *IQ and Human Intelligence* (Oxford University Press, 1998).

2. Robert Sternberg, George Forsythe, Jennifer Hedlund, Joseph Horvath, Richard Wagner, Wendy Williams, Scott Snook, and Elena Grigorenko, *Practical Intelligence in Everyday Life* (Cambridge University Press, 2000).

3. Peter Drucker, *The Practice of Management* (HarperBusiness 1993); Peter Drucker, "The New Productivity Challenge," *Harvard Business Review*, November 2001; Peter Drucker, *Managing in the Next Society* (Truman Talley Books, 2002); Henry Mintzberg, *Mintzberg on Management* (Free Press, 1989); John Kotter, "What Effective General Managers Really Do," *Harvard Business Review*, March 1999; Jim Collins and Jerry Porras, "Building Your Company's Vision," *Harvard Business Review*, September 1996; Jim Collins, "Level 5 Leadership: The Triumph of Humility and Fierce Resolve," *Harvard Business Review*, January 2001; Jack Welch with John Bryne, *Straight from the Gut* (Warner Books, 2001); Jim Collins, *Good to Great* (HarperBusiness, 2001); Alec Fisher and Michael Scriven, *Critical Thinking* (Edgepress, 1997); Sydney Finkelstein, *Why Smart Executives Fail* (Penguin Publishing, 2003); Mihaly Csikszentmihalya, *Creativity* (HarperCollins, 1996); Quinn Spitzer and Ron Evans, *Heads You Win* (Simon and Schuster, 1997); Larry Bossidy and Ram Charan, *Execution* (Crown Business, 2002).

4. Peter Drucker, *Managing in the Next Society* (Truman Talley Books, 2002); Henry Mintzberg, *Mintzberg on Management* (Free Press, 1989); John Kotter, "What Effective General Managers Really Do," *Harvard Business Review*, March 1999; Jim Collins, "Level 5 Leadership: The Triumph of Humility and Fierce Resolve," *Harvard Business Review*, January 2001; Robert Sternberg, *Successful Intelligence* (Plume Books, 1997); Peter Salovey and David Pizarro, "The Value of Emotional Intelligence," in *Models of Intelligence* (American Psychological Association Press, 2003); John Kihlstrom and Nancy Cantor, "Social Intelligence," in *Handbook of Intelligence*, ed. Robert Sternberg, (Cambridge University Press, 2000); Corinne Kosmitzki and Oliver John, "The Implicit Use of Explicit Conceptions of Social Intelligence," *Person Individual Differences*, 15, no. 1, (1993): pp. 11–23; Stephen J. Zaccaro, Janelle A. Gilbert, Kirk K. Thor, and Michael D. Mumford, "Leadership and Social Intelligence: Linking Social Perspectives and Behavioral Flexibility to Leader Effectiveness," *Leadership Quarterly*, 2, no. 4 (Winter 1991): pp. 317–342; John D. Mayer and Peter Salovey, "The Intelligence of Emotional Intelligence," *Intelligence*, 17, no. 4 (October–December 1993): 17(4), pp. 433–442.

5. Peter Drucker, "The New Productivity Challenge," *Harvard Business Review*, November 2001; Jim Collins and Jerry Porras, "Building Your Company's Vision," *Harvard Business Review*, September 1996; Henry Mintzberg, *Mintzberg on Management* (Free Press, 1989); Jim Collins, "Level 5 Leadership: The Triumph of Humility and Fierce Resolve," *Harvard Business Review*, January 2001; Alec Fisher and Michael Scriven, *Critical Thinking* (Edgepress, 1997); Jim Collins, *Good to Great* (HarperBusiness, 2001); Robert Sternberg, *Successful Intelligence* (Plume Books, 1997); Sydney Finkelstein, *Why Smart Executives Fail* (Penguin Publishing, 2003); Mihaly Csikszentmihalya, *Creativity* (HarperCollins, 1996); Jack Welch with John Bryne, *Straight from the Gut* (Warner Books, 2001); Gerald Matthews, Moshe Zeidner, and Richard

Roberts, *Emotional Intelligence* (MIT Press, 2002); Larry Bossidy and Ram Charan, *Execution* (Crown Business, 2002).

6. Alec Fisher and Michael Scriven, *Critical Thinking* (Edgepress, 1997).

7. Robert Kennedy, *Thirteen Days* (W.W. Norton, 1971).

8. Robert Kennedy, *Thirteen Days* (W.W. Norton, 1971) p. 38.

9. Robert Kennedy, *Thirteen Days* (W.W. Norton, 1971).

10. "Red Cross Defends Handling of Sept. 11 Donations," November 6, 2001, http://archives.cnn.com/2001/US/11/06/rec.charity.hearing, editorial staff, "Red Cross Caught Red-Handed," *Washing Times*, November 13, 2001.

11. Keith H. Hammonds, "How to Play Beane Ball," *Fast Company*, May 2003.

12. Michael Lewis, *Moneyball* (W.W. Norton, 1994).

## Chapter 4

1. Jim Collins, *Good to Great* (HarperBusiness, 2001).

2. Jack Welch with John Bryne, *Straight from the Gut* (Warner Books, 2001).

3. Peter Drucker, *Managing in the Next Society* (Truman Talley Books, 2002).

4. Peter Drucker, *Managing in the Next Society* (Truman Talley Books, 2002).

5. Jim Collins, *Good to Great* (HarperBusiness, 2001).

6. Peter Senge, *The Fifth Discipline* (Doubleday, 1990).

7. Mihaly Csikszentmihalya, *Creativity* (HarperCollins, 1996).

8. Mihaly Csikszentmihalya, *Creativity* (HarperCollins, 1996).

9. Justin Kruger and David Dunning, "Unskilled and Unaware of It," *Journal of*

*Personality and Social Psychology,* 77, no. 6 (1999): pp. 1121–1134.

10. Mihaly Csikszentmihalya, *Creativity* (HarperCollins, 1996).

## Chapter 5

1. Larry Bossidy and Ram Charan, *Execution* (Crown Business, 2002) p. 25.

2. Larry Bossidy and Ram Charan, *Execution* (Crown Business, 2002) p. 25.

3. Larry Bossidy and Ram Charan, *Execution* (Crown Business, 2002).

## Chapter 6

1. Katrina Brooker, "Jim Kilts Is an Old-School Curmudgeon," *Fortune*, December 30, 2002, p. 3.

2. Quinn Spitzer and Ron Evans, *Heads You Win* (Simon and Schuster, 1997).

3. Justin Kruger and David Dunning, "Unskilled and Unaware of It," *Journal of Personality and Social Psychology,* 77, no. 6 (1999): pp. 1121–1134.

4. Sydney Finkelstein, *Why Smart Executives Fail* (Penguin, 2003).

5. Ian Mitroff, *Smart Thinking for Crazy Times* (Berrett-Koehler Publishers, 1998).

6. Henry Mintzberg, *The Nature of Managerial Work* (HarperCollins, 1973).

7. Daniel Isenberg, "How Senior Managers Think," *Harvard Business Review*. November-December, 1984.

8. Daniel Isenberg, "Thinking and Managing: A Verbal Protocol Analysis of Managerial Problem Solving," *Academy of Management Journal,* 29, no. 4 (1986): pp. 775–788.

9. Karen Jehn and Keith Weigelt, "Reflective Versus Expedient Decision Making: Views from East and West," in *Wharton on Making Decisions*, ed. Stephen Hoch and Howard Kunreuther (John Wiley and Sons, 2001).

10. Quinn Spitzer and Ron Evans, *Heads You Win* (Simon and Schuster, 1997).

11. Hampton Sides, *Ghost Soldiers* (First Anchor Books, 2001).

12. Hampton Sides, *Ghost Soldiers* (First Anchor Books, 2001) p. 293.

13. Jim Collins, *Good to Great* (HarperBusiness, 2001).

14. Quinn Spitzer and Ron Evans, *Heads You Win* (Simon and Schuster, 1997).

15. Quinn Spitzer and Ron Evans, *Heads You Win* (Simon and Schuster, 1997).

## Chapter 7

1. Jeremy Campbell, *Improbable Machine* (Touchstone Books, 1990).

2. Jeremy Campbell, *Improbable Machine* (Touchstone Books, 1990).

3. R. Revlin, V. Leirer, H. Yopp, and R. Yopp, "The Belief Bias Effect in Formal Reasoning: The Influence of Knowledge on Logic," *Memory and Cognition*, 8 (1980): pp. 584–592.

4. Jeremy Campbell, *Improbable Machine* (Touchstone Books, 1990).

5. Jeremy Campbell, *Improbable Machine* (Touchstone Books, 1990).

6. Jeremy Campbell, *Improbable Machine* (Touchstone Books, 1990).

7. Jeremy Campbell, *Improbable Machine* (Touchstone Books, 1990).

8. Jeremy Campbell, *Improbable Machine* (Touchstone Books, 1990).

9. Jeremy Campbell, *Improbable Machine* (Touchstone Books, 1990).

10. Stephen Hoch, "Combining Models with Intuition to Improve Decisions," in *Wharton on Making Decisions*, eds. Stephen Hoch and Howard Kunreuther (John Wiley, 2001) p. 81.

11. J. Edward Russo and Paul Schoemaker, *Winning Decisions* (Doubleday, 2002).

12. J. Edward Russo and Paul Schoemaker, *Winning Decisions* (Doubleday, 2002).

13. Amos Tversky and Daniel Kahneman, "Judgments of and by Representativeness," in *Judgment Under Uncertainty*, ed. Kahneman Paul Slovic and Amos Tversky (1982, pp. 84–98).

14. Clifford Mottaz, "The Relative Importance of Intrinsic and Extrinsic Rewards as Determinants of Work Satisfaction," *Sociological Quarterly*, 26, no. 3 (Fall 1985): pp. 365–385.

15. J. Edward Russo and Paul Schoemaker, *Winning Decisions* (Doubleday, 2002).

16. J. Edward Russo and Paul Schoemaker, *Winning Decisions* (Doubleday, 2002).

17. Stephen Hoch, "Combining Models with Intuition to Improve Decisions," in *Wharton on Making Decisions*, eds. Stephen Hoch and Howard Kunreuther (John Wiley, 2001).

## Chapter 8

1. Edwin Boring, *The New Republic*, June 6, 1923, p. 35, "Intelligence as the tests test it"

2. Thorndike, E.L., "Intelligence and Its Measurement: A Symposium," *Journal of Educational Psychology*, vol. 12, (March-May 1921).

3. N.J. Mackintosh, *IQ and Human Intelligence* (Oxford University Press, 1998).

4. Robert Sternberg, George Forsythe, Jennifer Hedlund, Joseph Horvath, Richard Wagner, Wendy Williams, Scott Snook, and Elena Grigorenko, *Practical Intelligence in Everyday Life* (Cambridge University Press, 2000).

5. N.J. Mackintosh, *IQ and Human Intelligence* (Oxford University Press, 1998).

6. N.J. Mackintosh, *IQ and Human Intelligence* (Oxford University Press, 1998).

7. Robert Sternberg, George Forsythe, Jennifer Hedlund, Joseph Horvath, Richard Wagner, Wendy Williams, Scott Snook, and Elena

Grigorenko, *Practical Intelligence in Everyday Life* (Cambridge University Press, 2000).

8. N.J. Mackintosh, *IQ and Human Intelligence* (Oxford University Press, 1998).

9. John Hunter and Ronda Hunter, "Validity and Utility of Alternate Predictors of Job Performance," *Psychological Bulletin,* 96, no. 1 (July 1984): pp. 72–98; John Hunter, "Cognitive Ability, Cognitive Aptitudes, Job Knowledge, and Job Performance," *Journal of Vocational Behavior,* 29 (1986): pp. 340–362; John Hunter and Frank Schmidt, "Intelligence and Job Performance," *Psychology, Public Policy and Law,* 2 (1996): pp. 447–472; Frank Schmidt and John Hunter, "General Mental Ability in the World of Work: Occupational Attainment and Job Performance," *Journal of Personality and Social Psychology,* 86, no. 1 (2004): pp. 162–173.

10. Frank Schmidt and John Hunter, "General Mental Ability in the World of Work: Occupational Attainment and Job Performance," *Journal of Personality and Social Psychology,* 86, no. 1 (2004): pp. 162–173.

11. Frank Schmidt and John Hunter, "General Mental Ability in the World of Work: Occupational Attainment and Job Performance," *Journal of Personality and Social Psychology,* 86, no. 1 (2004): pp. 162–173.

12. John Hunter and Ronda Hunter, "Validity and Utility of Alternate Predictors of Job Performance," *Psychological Bulletin,* 96, no. 1 (July 1984): pp. 72–98.

13. Jesus Salgado, Neil Anderson, Silvia Moscoso, Cristina Bertua, Filip de Fruyt, and Jean Pierre Rolland," A Meta-analytic Study of General Mental Ability Validity for Different Occupations in the European Community," *Journal of Applied Psychology,* 88 (2003): pp. 1068–1081.

14. Robert Sternberg, George Forsythe, Jennifer Hedlund, Joseph Horvath, Richard Wagner, Wendy Williams, Scott Snook, and Elena Grigorenko, *Practical Intelligence in Everyday Life* (Cambridge University Press, 2000).

15. Robert Sternberg, George Forsythe, Jennifer Hedlund, Joseph Horvath, Richard Wagner, Wendy Williams, Scott Snook, and Elena Grigorenko, *Practical Intelligence in Everyday Life* (Cambridge University Press, 2000).

16. *Wonderlic Personnel Test Users Manual* (Wonderlic Inc., 2000).

## Chapter 9

1. B. Leuner, "Emotional intelligence and Emancipation," *Praxis der Kinderpsychologie und Kinderpsychiatrie* 15 (1966): pp. 196–203.

2. Wayne Payne, "A Study of Emotion: Developing Emotional Intelligence; Self-Integration; Relating to Fear, Pain, and Desire," *Dissertation Abstracts International,* 47 (1985): p. 203.

3. Daniel Goleman, *Emotional Intelligence* (1985) (Bantam, 1995) p. 34.

4. Gerald Matthews, Moshe Zeidner, and Richard Roberts, *Emotional Intelligence* (MIT Press, 2002).

5. Peter Salovey and David Pizarro "The Value of Emotional Intelligence," in *Models of Intelligence* (APA 2003).

6. Richard Mayer, Peter Salovey, R. Sternberg, J. Loutrey, T. Lubart, and David Caruso, "Models of Emotional Intelligence," in *Handbook of Intelligence,* ed. Robert Sternberg (Cambridge University Press, 2000).

7. M. Davies, L. Stankov, and R. Roberts, "Emotional Intelligence: In Search of an Elusive Construct," *Journal of Personality and Social Psychology,* 44 (1998): pp. 113–126; J. Mayer, P. Salovey, D. Caruso, "Competing Models of Emotional Intelligence," in *Handbook of Human Intelligence* (2nd ed.), ed. Robert Sternberg (Cambridge University Press, 2000).

8. Gerald Matthews, Moshe Zeidner, and Richard Roberts, *Emotional Intelligence* (MIT Press, 2002).

9. Murray R. Barrick and Michael K. Mount, "The Big Five Personality Dimensions and Job Performance: A Meta-analysis," *Personnel Psychology,* 44, no. 1 (Spring 1991): pp. 1–26.

10. Jesus Salgado, Neil Anderson, Silvia Moscoso, Cristina Bertua, Filip de Fruyt, and Jean Pierre Rolland, "A Meta-analytic Study of General Mental Ability Validity for Different Occupations in the European Community," *Journal of Applied Psychology,* 88 (2003): pp. 1068–1081.

11. Jay Conger, "Max Weber's Conceptualization of Charismatic Authority: Its Influence on Organizational Research," *Leadership Quarterly,* vol. 4 (April 1993): p. 282.

12. Max Weber, *Economy and Society,* vol. 1, eds. G. Roth and C. Wittich [originally published 1925], p. 241 (Bedminster, 1968).

13. Max Weber, *Economy and Society,* vol. 1, eds. G. Roth and C. Wittich [originally published 1925], p. 241 (Bedminster, 1968).

14. Bruce J. Avolio and Bernard M. Bass, "Individual Consideration Viewed at Multiple Levels of Analysis: A Multi-level Framework for Examining the Diffusion of Transformational Leadership," *Leadership Quarterly,* 6, no. 2 (Summer 1995): pp. 199–218; Jay Conger and Rabindra Kanungo, *Charismatic leadership in Organizations* (Sage Publications, 1998).

15. Rakesh Khurana, *Searching for a Corporate Savior: The Irrational Quest for Charismatic CEOs* (Princeton University Press, 2002) p. XI.

16. Jim Collins, *Good to Great* (HarperBusiness, 2001).

17. Mihaly Csikszentmihalya, *Creativity* (HarperCollins, 1996).

18. Mihaly Csikszentmihalya, *Creativity* (HarperCollins, 1996) p. 51.

19. Robert Langreth, "Reviving Novartis," *Forbes,* February 5, 2001.

20. Robert Langreth, "Reviving Novartis," *Forbes,* February 5, 2001.

21. Murray R. Barrick and Michael K. Mount, "The Big Five Personality Dimensions and Job Performance: A Meta-analysis," *Personnel Psychology,* 44, no. 1 (Spring 1991) pp. 1–26.

22. R. J. House, "A 1976 Theory of Charismatic Leadership," in *Leadership: The Cutting Edge,* eds. J.G. Hunt and L.L. Larson (Southern Illinois University Press, 1977).

23. Daniel Goleman, Richard Boyatzis, and Annie McKee, *Primal Leadership* (Harvard University Press 2002) p. 27.

24. Peter Drucker, *Managing in the Next Society* (Truman Talley Books, 2002) p. 89.

25. Jim Collins, *Good to Great* (HarperBusiness, 2001) p. 13.

## Chapter 10

1. Michael Scriven, *Evaluation Thesaurus* (Sage Publications, 1991).

2. Murray R. Barrick and Michael K. Mount, "The Big Five Personality Dimensions and Job Performance: A Meta-analysis," *Personnel Psychology,* 44, no. 1 (Spring 1991): pp. 1–26.

## Chapter 11

1. Ralph Wagner, "The Employment Interview: A Critical Summary," *Personnel Psychology,* 2 (1949).

2. W. D. Scott, "Scientific Selection of Salesmen," *Advertising and Selling Magazine,* October 1915.

3. W. D. Scott, "Selection of Employees by Means of Quantitative Determinations," *Annals of the American Academy of Political and Social Sciences,* 65 (1916); W. D. Scott, W. V. Bingham, and G.M. Whipple, "Scientific Selection of Salesmen," *Salemanship,* 4 (1916): pp. 106–108.

4. Egbert Magson, *How We Judge Intelligence* (Cambridge University Press, 1914) p. 1.

5. Egbert Magson, *How We Judge Intelligence* (Cambridge University Press, 1914) p. 29.

6. E. F. Wonderlic, "Improving Interview Technique," *Personnel,* 18 (1942): p. 232.

7. Edwin Ghiselli, "The Validity of a Personnel Interview," *Personnel Psychology,* 19, no. 4 (1966): pp. 389–394.

8. Edwin Ghiselli, "The Validity of a Personnel Interview," *Personnel Psychology,* 19, no. 4 (1966): pp. 389–394.

9. Stephan J. Motowidlo, Gary W. Carter, Marvin D. Dunnette, and Nancy Tippins, "Studies of the Structured Behavioral Interview," *Journal of Applied Psychology,* 77, no. 5 (October 1992): pp. 571–587.

10. Robert Eder, K. Michele Kacmar, and Gerald Ferris, "Employment Interview Research: History and Synthesis," in *The Employment Interview*, eds. Robert Eder and Gerald Ferris (1989, Sage Publications).

11. Stephan J. Motowidlo, Gary W. Carter, Marvin D. Dunnette, and Nancy Tippins, "Studies of the Structured Behavioral Interview," *Journal of Applied Psychology,* 77, no. 5 (October 1992): pp. 571–587.

12. Stephan J. Motowidlo, Gary W. Carter, Marvin D. Dunnette, and Nancy Tippins, "Studies of the Structured Behavioral Interview," *Journal of Applied Psychology,* 77, no. 5 (October 1992): pp. 571–587.

## Chapter 12

1. Mark R. Anderson, M.D., "A Short History of Scurvy," ©2000, http://www.riparia.org/scurvy_hx.htm.

2. "Vitamin C," http://en.wikipedia.org/wiki/Vitamin_C.

3. Kristen Philipkowski, "Show Time for Stem-cell Science," *Wired News*, November 10, 2004.

4. Stephan J. Motowidlo, Gary W. Carter, Marvin D. Dunnette, and Nancy Tippins, "Studies of the Structured Behavioral Interview," *Journal of Applied Psychology,* 77, no. 5 (October 1992): pp. 571–587.

5. Jesus Salgado, Neil Anderson, Silvia Moscoso, Cristina Bertua, Filip de Fruyt, and Jean Pierre Rolland, "A Meta-analytic Study of General Mental Validity for Different Occupations in the European Community," *Journal of Applied Psychology,* 88 (2003): pp. 1068–1081.

6. John Hunter and Ronda Hunter, "Validity and Utility of Alternate Predictors of Job Performance," *Psychological Bulletin,* 96, no. 1 (July 1984): pp. 72–98; Jesus Salgado, Neil Anderson, Silvia Moscoso, Cristina Bertua, Filip de Fruyt, and Jean Pierre Rolland, "A Meta-analytic Study of General Mental Ability Validity for Different Occupations in the European Community," *Journal of Applied Psychology,* 88 (2003): pp. 1068–1081; Frank Schmidt and John Hunter, "General Mental Ability in the World of Work: Occupational Attainment and Job Performance," *Journal of Personality and Social Psychology,* 86 (2004): pp. 162–173.

7. Jesus F. Salgado and Silvia Moscoso, "Comprehensive Meta-analysis of the Construct Validity of the Employment Interview," *European Journal of Work and Organizational Psychology,* 11, no. 3 (September 2002): pp. 299–324.

8. Allen I. Huffcutt, Philip L. Roth, Michael A. McDaniel, "A Meta-analytic Investigation of Cognitive Ability in Employment Interview Evaluations: Moderating Characteristics and Implications for Incremental Validity," *Journal of Applied Psychology,* 81, no. 5 (October 1996): pp. 459–473.

9. Jesus Salgado and Silvia Moscoso, "Comprehensive Meta-analysis of the Construct Validity of the Employment Interview," *European Journal of Work and Organizational Psychology,* 11, no. 3 (September 2002): pp. 299–324.

## Chapter 13

1. Joseph Fagan III, "A Theory of Intelligence as Processing," *Psychology, Public Policy and Law,* 6 (2000): p. 168.

## Chapter 14

1. Robert Sternberg, *Beyond IQ* (Cambridge University Press, 1985) p. 68.

2. Sample questions adapted from intelligencetest.com, 2005, http://www.intelligencetest.com/questions.htm name of site:IQ test labs

3. Peter Drucker, *The Practice of Management* (HarperBusiness, 1993); Peter Drucker, "The New Productivity Challenge," *Harvard Business Review*, November 2001; Peter Drucker, *Managing in the Next Society* (Truman Talley Books, 2002); Henry Mintzberg, *Mintzberg on Management* (Free Press, 1989); John Kotter, "What Effective General Managers Really Do," *Harvard Business Review*, March 1999; Jim Collins and Jerry Porras, "Building Your Company's Vision," *Harvard Business Review*, September 1996; Jim Collins, "Level 5 Leadership: The Triumph of Humility and Fierce Resolve," *Harvard Business Review*, January 2001; Jack Welch with John Byrne, *Straight from the Gut* (Warner Books, 2001); Jim Collins, *Good to Great* (HarperBusiness, 2001); Alec Fisher and Michael Scriven, *Critical Thinking* (Edgepress, 1997); Sydney Finkelstein, *Why Smart Executives Fail* (Penguin, 2003); Mihaly Csikszentmihalya, *Creativity* (Harper Collins, 1996); Quinn Spitzer and Ron Evans, *Heads You Win* (Simon and Schuster, 1997); Larry Bossidy and Ram Charan, *Execution* (Crown Business, 2002).

4. Peter Drucker, *Managing in the Next Society* (Truman Talley Books, 2002); Henry Mintzberg, *Mintzberg on Management* (Free Press, 1989); John Kotter, "What Effective General Managers Really Do," *Harvard Business Review*, March 1999; Jim Collins, "Level 5 Leadership: The Triumph of Humility and Fierce Resolve," *Harvard Business Review*, January 2001; Robert Sternberg, *Successful Intelligence* (Plume Books, 1997); Peter Salovey and David Pizarro, "The Value of Emotional Intelligence," in *Models of Intelligence* (American Psychological Association Press, 2003); John Kihlstrom and Nancy Cantor,

"Social Intelligences," in *Handbook of Intelligence*, ed. Robert Sternberg (Cambridge University Press, 2000); Corinne Kosmitzki and Oliver John, "The Implicit Use of Explicit Conceptions of Social Intelligence," *Person Individual Differences*, 15, no. 1 (1993): pp. 11–23; Stephen J. Zaccaro, Janelle A. Gilbert, Kirk K. Thor, and Michael D. Mumford, "Leadership and Social Intelligence: Linking Social Perspectives and Behavioral Flexibility to Leader Effectiveness," *Leadership Quarterly*, 2, no. 4 (Winter 1991): pp. 317–342; John D. Mayer and Peter Salovey, "The Intelligence of Emotional Intelligence," *Intelligence*, 17, no. 4 (October—December 1993): pp. 433–442.

5. Peter Drucker, "The New Productivity Challenge," *Harvard Business Review*, November 2001; Jim Collins and Jerry Porras, "Building Your Company's Vision," *Harvard Business Review*, September 1996; Henry Mintzberg, *Mintzberg on Management* (Free Press, 1989); Jim Collins, "Level 5 Leadership: The Triumph of Humility and Fierce Resolve," *Harvard Business Review*, January 2001; Alec Fisher and Michael Scriven, *Critical Thinking* (Edgepress, 1997); Jim Collins, *Good to Great* (HarperBusiness, 2001); Robert Sternberg, *Successful Intelligence* (Plume Books, 1997); Sydney Finkelstein, *Why Smart Executives Fail* (Penguin, 2003); Mihaly Csikszentmihalya, *Creativity* (Harper Collins, 1996); Jack Welch with John Byrne, *Straight from the Gut* (Warner Books, 2001); Gerald Matthews, Moshe Zeidner, and Richard Roberts, *Emotional Intelligence* (MIT Press, 2002); Larry Bossidy and Ram Charan, *Execution* (Crown Business, 2002).

6. R. Sternberg, M. Ferrari, P. Clinkenbeard, and E. Grigorenko, "Identification, Instruction, and Assessment of Gifted Children: A Construct Validation of a Triarchic Model," *Gifted Child Quarterly*, 40: pp. 129–137; R. Sternberg, E. Grigorenko, M. Ferrari, and P. Clinkenbeard, "A Triarchic Analysis of an Aptitude-Treatment Interaction," *European Journal of Psychological Assessment*, 15 (1999): pp. 1–11.

7. Peter Bycio, Kenneth Alvares, and June Hahn, "Situational Specificity in Assessment Center Ratings: A Confirmatory Factor Analysis," *Journal of Applied Psychology,* 72 (1987): pp. 463–474.

8. Peter Bycio, Kenneth Alvares, and June Hahn, "Situational Specificity in Assessment Center Ratings: A Confirmatory Factor Analysis," *Journal of Applied Psychology,* 72 (1987): p. 473.

9. Alec Fisher and Michael Scriven, *Critical Thinking* (Edgepress, 1997).

10. Stephan J. Motowidlo, Gary W. Carter, Marvin D. Dunnette, and Nancy Tippins, "Studies of the Structured Behavioral Interview," *Journal of Applied Psychology,* 77, no. 5 (October 1992): pp. 571–587.

## Chapter 15

1. Christopher Cerf and Victor Navasky, *The Experts Speak* (Random House, 1998) p. 227.

2. Christopher Cerf and Victor Navasky, *The Experts Speak* (Random House, 1998) p. 226.

3. Christopher Cerf and Victor Navasky, *The Experts Speak* (Random House, 1998) p. 231.

4. Justin Menkes, "What Do Structured Interviews Actually Measure? A Construct Validity Study," *Dissertation Abstracts International: Section B: The Sciences and Engineering,* 63, no. 3-B (September 2002).

5. Study conducted by Justin Menkes, 2003, peer reviewed by The Evaluation Center, Western Michigan.

6. Jennifer Palthe, "Evaluation Report: The Validity and Reliability of the ExI Assessment Instrument," The Evaluation Center, Western Michigan University, February, 2004, p. 9.

## Chapter 16

1. Richard Hernstein, Raymond Nickerson, Margarita de Sanchez, and John Swets, "Teaching Thinking Skills," *American Psychologist,* vol. 41 (November 1986).

2. Richard Hernstein, Raymond Nickerson, Margarita de Sanchez, and John Swets, "Teaching Thinking Skills," *American Psychologist* (1986) vol. 41, p. 1279.

3. Tim van Gelder and Melanie Bissett, "Cultivating Expertise in Informal Reasoning," *Canadian Journal of Experimental Psychology,* vol. 58, (June 2004): pp. 142–152.

4. Robert Swartz and D. N. Perkins, *Teaching Thinking: Issues and Approaches* (Midwest Publications, 1990); Howard Gardner, *The Unschooled Mind* (Basic Books, 1995).

5. Alec Fisher, *Critical Thinking* (Cambridge University Press, 2001).

6. Robert Swartz and D. N. Perkins, *Teaching Thinking: Issues and Approaches* (Midwest Publications, 1990); Howard Gardner, *The Unschooled Mind* (Basic Books, 1995).

7. M. Rowe, "Wait Time and Rewards as Instructional Variables: Their Influence on Language, Logic and Fate Control," *Journal of Research in Science Teaching,* 11 (1974): pp. 81–94.

8. Diane Halpern, "Teaching Critical Thinking for Transfer Across Domains," *American Psychologist,* April 1998, p. 455.

## Chapter 17

1. Ichak Adizes, *Managing Corporate Lifecycles* (Adizes Institute Publishing, 2004).

# Index

# About the Author

Justin Menkes is a Managing Director of the Executive Intelligence Group, a leading provider of executive assessment services to major corporations around the globe. The firm is an exclusive partner of Spencer Stuart, the world's preeminent executive search firm. Executive Intelligence Group's clients include Texas Pacific Group (TPG), Dupont, Pratt & Whitney, and Unilever. Menkes created the proprietary Executive Intelligence Evaluation, used by businesses to identify, develop, and hire effective leaders for their organizations. Menkes is nationally recognized for his expertise in managerial assessment; he has been cited by Malcolm Gladwell for his work on intelligence and has trained other psychologists in best practice techniques. He has written for the *Harvard Business Review*, and served as an adviser to McKinsey and Company for its best-selling book *The War for Talent*. Menkes earned a Ph.D. in organizational behavior from Claremont Graduate University, where he studied with Peter Drucker, Michael Scriven, and Mihaly Csikszentmihalyi. He has an M.A. in psychology from the University of Pennsylvania and a B.A. from Haverford College. He lives in Los Angeles.

# About the Executive Intelligence Group

Executive Intelligence Group (EIG) was founded by Justin Menkes and Robert Stark in 2002. The two have worked in the executive assessment field since the early 1990s. As Managing Directors of EIG, they lead a team of expert consultants that advise business leaders on executive selection and promotion decisions. Executive Intelligence Group is the exclusive executive assessment partner of Spencer Stuart, the leading privately held, global executive search firm.